The College Survival Guide

Navigating Academics, Social Experiences, and Daily Life from Your Freshman Year and Beyond

© Copyright 2024 - All rights reserved.

The content contained within this book may not be reproduced, duplicated, or transmitted without direct written permission from the author or the publisher.

Under no circumstances will any blame or legal responsibility be held against the publisher or author for any damages, reparation, or monetary loss due to the information contained within this book, either directly or indirectly.

Legal Notice:

This book is copyright-protected. It is only for personal use. You cannot amend, distribute, sell, use, quote, or paraphrase any part of the content within this book without the consent of the author or publisher.

Disclaimer Notice:

Please note the information contained within this document is for educational and entertainment purposes only. All effort has been executed to present accurate, up-to-date, reliable, and complete information. No warranties of any kind are declared or implied. Readers acknowledge that the author is not engaging in the rendering of legal, financial, medical, or professional advice. The content within this book has been derived from various sources. Please consult a licensed professional before attempting any techniques outlined in this book.

By reading this document, the reader agrees that under no circumstances is the author responsible for any losses, direct or indirect, that are incurred as a result of the use of the information contained within this document, including, but not limited to, errors, omissions, or inaccuracies.

Table of Contents

INTRODUCTION 1
CHAPTER 1: FRESHMAN FOLLIES: SURVIVING YOUR FIRST YEAR WITH FLAIR 2
CHAPTER 2: STUDY SMARTS: ACE YOUR CLASSES WITHOUT LOSING YOUR MIND 9
CHAPTER 3: DORM ROOM DIPLOMACY: LIVING IN HARMONY WITH ROOMMATES 18
CHAPTER 4: NAVIGATING NUTRITION ON CAMPUS 26
CHAPTER 5: BALANCING FUN AND STUDIES 33
CHAPTER 6: STRATEGIES FOR TEST-TAKING AND STRESS-BUSTING 40
CHAPTER 7: MAKING FRIENDS AND INFLUENCING PEOPLE 48
CHAPTER 8: BUDGETING BLISS: MANAGING MONEY WITHOUT MISSING OUT 56
CHAPTER 9: INTERNSHIP INSIGHTS: GAINING EXPERIENCE WHILE IN SCHOOL 65
CHAPTER 10: SENIOR YEAR SPRINT: PREPARING FOR LIFE AFTER GRADUATION 72
CONCLUSION 81
CHECK OUT ANOTHER BOOK IN THE SERIES 83
REFERENCES 84

Introduction

Did you just ace your college applications and score a spot at your dream school? Are you excited about college life? Freedom, dorm life, late-night adventures – it's all just around the corner. Can you already picture grabbing lunch with new friends? Imagine finally being free from the rules that govern your family home. College life is about to be epic. Are you worried about getting stuck with someone who doesn't vibe with you? Don't worry. This guide will help you navigate that – and everything else college throws your way. Buckle up, college star.

Stepping onto a college campus is like entering a whole new world. It's exciting, overwhelming, and probably a little scary. There's a lot to navigate between classes, making new friends, and figuring out the best places to eat. If you're living in a dorm room for the first time, sharing your space with a complete stranger can add a whole new layer of challenges.

This book is your guide to thriving in college. Among other things, you'll be equipped with the tools you need to master the material, manage your time effectively, and avoid those late-night cram sessions. You will learn how to create a schedule that lets you enjoy the social side of college without sacrificing your grades, stretch your money further so you can still afford that occasional pizza with friends, and turn your dorm room into a breeding ground for amazing college memories.

Unlike other books about college life that are filled with complicated jargon and generic advice, the College Survival Guide speaks your language. As a busy soon-to-be college student, what you need is a book written in clear and concise language. This easy-to-understand guide is packed with practical tips and tricks to help you conquer everything from dorm room diplomacy to deciphering your class schedule.

College isn't just about attending lectures and hitting the books (although those are important, too). It's also about exploring your interests, making lifelong friends, and maybe even catching a few winks of sleep. This book will teach you how to create a balanced schedule that allows you to excel in your classes while still having a vibrant social life and taking care of yourself.

Are you ready to go from feeling like a lost freshman to a confident college student who thrives both inside and outside the classroom? Then, keep reading. Everything has a beginning, and college life marks the beginning of the rest of your life as an adult. Good luck.

Chapter 1: Freshman Follies: Surviving Your First Year with Flair

After reading this chapter, you'll learn everything you need to know before you set foot in college. You'll gain insight into the initial challenges you might face and how to navigate them. You'll understand that with the right mindset, you can transform these hurdles into opportunities. University life comes with substantial new responsibilities. However, if you know what to expect and keep a positive mindset all the way through, you'll develop skills such as time and stress management, financial literacy, and mindfulness, which will help you throughout your life. You'll understand why participating in campus life and making friends will help you thrive and understand the significance of self-care in overcoming the difficulties that this transitional stage in life brings.

Having a positive mindset will help you navigate through college challenges.
https://www.pexels.com/photo/woman-studying-inside-the-classroom-7092336/

The Challenges You Might Face in College

Dealing with Homesickness

No matter how busy you keep yourself, the number of new friends you make, or even how happy and excited you are, you will likely feel homesick. Nothing will fill the gap left by your friends and family. Not only will you miss everyone in your life, but you'll also miss being in the comfort of your home and sleeping in your bed. Many people think they would be fine moving away, especially since they know that the move is temporary and that they will be back to visit on the holidays. However, most new college students are taken by surprise when they realize that it's harder than they thought it would be. Luckily, the symptoms of homesickness are alleviated in the digital age. While video calls don't live up to the real thing, they can still bridge the gap between you and your loved ones. Many students also find it comforting to decorate their rooms with personal items from back home.

Increased Responsibilities

High school is difficult, but a university comes with a different level of challenges. It will put your time management, stress management, critical thinking, research, communication, problem-solving, and collaboration skills to the test. Not only will you be expected to absorb great amounts of information, but you'll have to relate these concepts to the real world. You'll have more challenging classes and more projects and assignments.

Most college classes don't spoon-feed you information. In most cases, you'll have to figure things out on your own. You'll also be responsible for finding out when everything is due and managing your time. Try to make friends with people who take the same classes as you. This way, you can remind each other of deadlines, explain concepts or give study tips to one another, and form study groups. Depending on your professors, your success in certain courses depends on your note-taking abilities. If you make friends with people in your classes, you can share your notes with each other to fill in potential gaps. You'll also benefit from introducing yourself to your professors and attending office hours as needed or required. Professors appreciate students who put in the effort to learn and participate.

Issues with Roommates

Some university residence teams work hard to ensure that students are paired with roommates with whom they'll get along. However, no one is perfect. Even if you're lucky enough to get roommates that you like, you're bound to face some conflicts with them. To prevent arguments from arising, you can set some boundaries and ground rules to begin with. These agreements can outline how you split up your responsibilities, such as cleaning, rent, grocery shopping, cooking, and so on.

You can also discuss whether and when it's acceptable to have friends over, engage in potentially disturbing hobbies or interests like playing instruments or listening to music out loud, etc. If you're not compatible at all with your roommate or if issues that you can't work through arise, don't hesitate to discuss the problem with your residence life assistant or the person in charge. They will offer the assistance and support you need to solve the problem.

Discovering Effective Study Techniques

The study techniques you need to excel in universities may drastically differ from the ones you need in order to do well in school. A significant aspect of transitioning into this phase of your life is understanding the learning style that is most suitable for you. Some people learn best when explaining concepts out loud, some find that information sticks best when taking notes, and others benefit from cue cards. You also need to find your favorite place to study. While your room might seem like the obvious choice, many people get distracted when they're alone. Studying in a cozy and quiet coffee shop or in the library can leave you with no choice but to sit and focus. Many students also feel encouraged and hold themselves accountable when they study with others.

Time Management

Another important aspect of studying effectively is learning how to manage your time. Setting up a study schedule will help you avoid cramming everything on the night before your exam. Not only will time management help you thrive in the university, but it's also one of the most important life skills you'll ever learn. Time management is the key to balancing your work, university, social, and personal life. You can use tools like your phone's reminder app, online calendars, and physical to-do lists or planners to stay on top of your responsibilities. Note everything you need to do, including your classes, assignments, study sessions, extracurricular activities, work, social activities, chores, and everything in between.

Developing Financial Literacy

Financial literacy is a skill that will help you plan your future and excel in various aspects and stages of your life. You don't need to budget for every item that you spend your money on; however, you need to allocate certain amounts of money to different necessities, responsibilities, and activities. Knowing where your money goes can help you track it and avoid exceeding your spending limit for unnecessary activities, such as shopping or going out with your friends. The most important thing to do when it comes to finances is to understand the difference between your wants and needs. Needs should always come first, and in most cases, they can't be put off. Wants, however, can be delayed.

You can also experiment with different budgeting methods, such as the 50-30-20 rule, which suggests that you spend 50% of your income on your needs, 30% on your wants, and save the rest – or the 40-40-20 rule, which suggests that you save 40% of your income, set the other 40% aside for taxes, and spend the remaining 20% on your wants and needs. There is no right or wrong when it comes to budgeting. The most important thing is that you come up with a plan that accommodates your current lifestyle while offering a safety net for emergencies and future financial success. If that's unachievable, you might have to rethink your priorities and redefine your wants.

Navigating and Redefining Relationships

A university transforms several aspects of your life, including how you view and navigate relationships. After high school, you and your friends will each walk down your own path. You'll each enroll in different majors; some will choose to work right away, and a few will juggle work with study and even other extracurricular activities. You'll each be consumed by the unique responsibilities and events that life throws your way.

While a few friendships will stay strong, expect to lose many people along the way. While losing people whom you've known for years can be frightening and extremely frustrating, you'll make new friendships and experience numerous opportunities. The shift from high school to university life leaves you wondering who you really are. You start to question your interests, talents, and entire personality. During this time, you might be subjected to peer pressure and negative influences from others. This is why you must always love and put yourself above everyone else and avoid changing for anyone else.

In school, you are a big fish in a small pond – in a university, you're a small fish in a big pond, and during the life that follows, you'll be a small fish in an ocean. In other words, in school, you're surrounded by a small population of like-minded individuals, while in a university, you're surrounded by more people with completely different interests, more diverse backgrounds, yet somewhat similar upbringings, objectives, and motivations.

The older you grow, the more likely you'll have to deal with people with different morals, values, intentions, interests, goals, and backgrounds. Always make sure that you surround yourself with people who genuinely care for you, uplift and support you, and encourage you to become a better version of yourself. The people you make friends with can make or break your experience in a university, so try to make the best out of this once-in-a-lifetime experience.

Partying Right

It would be very unreasonable to advise you against partying unless you don't do it for personal reasons, which would be perfectly fine. Do the things you enjoy, but make sure to do them responsibly. If you end up with the wrong crowd, you might end up partying and drinking every night, which would eventually get in the way of your personal, social, and academic life. Always reflect on your goals, and don't lose sight of why you're enrolled in the university. Yes, you're there to have fun, but you're primarily there to build a great future for yourself. Be in charge of your actions and decisions, and define your limits and boundaries. Have fun, but do it with caution.

Maintaining Your Mental and Physical Health

Universities often offer a wide range of services and support, from physical and mental health services to counseling. The transition to a university can be extremely overwhelming, which is why you should consider making use of these services while you're there. The university is the right time to focus on building a bright future. There is so much to do and so many opportunities to chase, but don't let that compromise your health. Your well-being should always be a priority, so take proactive measures to make sure that your mental, emotional, and physical health is in good shape.

Costs of Education

Another common challenge that university students face is the cost of education and paying off their debts. It is often the only thing standing between students and their ability to receive quality higher education. Fortunately, several programs allow you to receive aid and grants for education. You can also implement effective time management techniques and seek out part-time job opportunities to help you pay for your tuition or repay your debts.

Common Mistakes to Avoid in College

Rushing to Room with Your Best Friend

Picture this: You and your best friend from high school are excited to finally move in together! You talk about all the fun you're going to have and all the things you're going to do when you earn your freedom. Surprisingly, you both take a slap in the face when you discover that being best friends doesn't necessarily mean that you're compatible as roommates. You discover that while you prefer to sleep in complete silence and darkness, they like to sleep with the lights on and can only drift off to sleep while listening to a podcast, or that while you like to keep the space clean, they have no problem with letting things get a little messy.

You might also learn that they don't care to participate in maintaining the space or notice that if you don't do all the chores by yourself, they won't get them done. Instead of risking ruining your friendship because you have different sleep, hygiene, and cleanliness habits, consider giving your assigned roommate on campus a chance, as it's a great way to expand your social circle.

Don't Rush to Adjust

It's great to start the university with high hopes and a positive attitude. That said, don't expect to hit the ground running. Some people are lucky enough to make friends and adjust to college life from day one; however, the majority of them take more time to do so. It might take you weeks into your first semester or even months before you start feeling connected and adjusting to college. Don't feel frustrated, and remember that you'll eventually find your crowd. You're neither in the wrong place nor are you not cut out for a university. Good things take time, and great things take even longer.

Get Out of Your Comfort Zone

During your first few weeks in college, cocooning in your dorm can feel like the obvious choice. You might only want to eat your comfort food and watch your favorite shows. As unappealing as it may sound, challenge yourself to dive into campus life. Explore all the clubs and extracurricular activities. Start creating memories and building friendships that will last you a lifetime. Remember that only you have the power to turn your situation upside down. You can choose to dwell on the fact that you don't fit in or make an active effort to find your community.

Don't Skip Classes

A university offers a new sense of freedom. No one is there to tell you that you must attend all your classes and nag you if you don't. Attending class, studying, and submitting your assignments on time are all up to you. Yes, it might be tempting to get a taste of your newfound freedom. However, you must remember that one skipped class can lead to a spiral of numerous missed lectures and accumulated content. It might be fun at first, but you'll finally end up feeling guilty as you approach the end of your semester.

Avoid Revenge Bedtime Procrastination

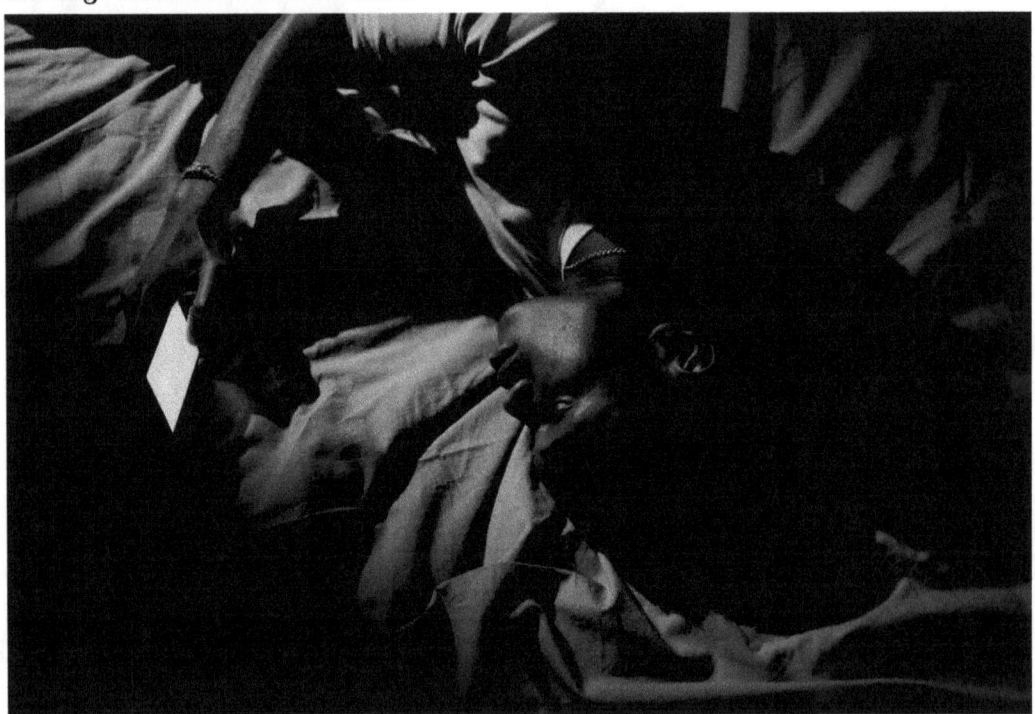

Your problems can be solved with effective time management rather than taking away your valuable sleep time.
https://www.pexels.com/photo/a-man-lying-on-the-bed-while-using-his-mobile-phone-6943426/

Everyone knows about work and study procrastination, but have you ever heard of revenge bedtime procrastination? Do you ever have so much to do every single day that you realize that going to bed early will leave you with no time for relaxation or entertainment, so you end up either sleeping very late or pulling all-nighters? As much as you might need time for yourself, bedtime procrastination can affect your physical and cognitive functions. Whether you have so much on your plate or need to engage in a fun activity, make sure to get enough quality sleep every night. Your problems can be solved with effective time management rather than taking away your valuable sleep time.

Don't Hesitate to Reach Out For Help

If you watched coming-of-age movies while growing up, then you've probably learned that seniors always make fun of freshmen in college. This, however, isn't always the case in the real world. Truth be said, there are bullies in college, just like everywhere else. However, the vast majority aren't going to be rude to you just because it's your first year in college. Many fellow students will be willing to help you whether you need directions or advice regarding one of your courses. Don't hesitate to reach out to your guidance counselor or professors either, as it's their job to help.

Why You Should Go Out of Your Way to Make Friends

Making friends and participating in campus life at a university isn't a leisure activity. It is crucial to your mental and emotional health, as well as your academic success. According to Cleveland University, students who make friends are more likely to perform well in academics and pass their courses to graduate on schedule. Even in majors that require a lot of time, focus, and effort, building relationships with others can be helpful. Making friends aids with stress management, which is needed for time management and cognitive function.

Friends in a university also make great study partners. They will offer the needed emotional support, motivation, and encouragement. You'll all celebrate milestones and achievements together and work hard to improve and stay on track. Positive friendships will ensure that you don't feel alone throughout your academic journey. They will also hold you accountable for thriving academically. Whenever you find it hard to approach others in college, remember that you're all in the same boat. You're all new to this experience, and most of you are struggling to adjust to this transitional phase in life. Take the step to introduce yourself and spark conversations with others. You never know – one of these initiatives might lead to an invaluable friendship that will last you a lifetime.

The Necessity of Self-Care

Practicing self-care is critical to your mental, emotional, and physical health at a university. This new phase in life comes with numerous novel responsibilities and commitments. The only way to stay afloat is to dedicate enough time to yourself. Prioritizing your needs, wants, and well-being is not selfish but is crucial to creating a healthy, enjoyable, and successful college experience.

In college, you commit to several classes and extracurriculars that leave you with little time to receive adequate sleep, balanced nutrition, exercise, enjoyment, and relaxation. Self-care is all about prioritizing your needs. You can prep your meals for the entire week on the weekends, create a rigid bedtime for yourself, dedicate at least half an hour of your day toward regular exercise, and try to integrate mindfulness techniques into your day. Catering to your body's basic needs ensures that you're energized enough to perform your tasks effectively.

When you're under constant stress, your body will go into survival mode. You'll struggle with burnout and brain fog, hindering your academic performance and your ability to enjoy your college experience. Engaging in self-care techniques can help you maintain a positive attitude, enhance your resilience, and alleviate mental strains. Opt to maintain a healthy balance between your personal life and your academic and extracurricular demands. Use time-management tools to dedicate time slots for your responsibilities. Avoid procrastination and aim to stick to your calendar. This will allow you to set boundaries and ensure that you have enough time for relaxation and leisure activities. Remember that you can't pour from an empty cup. How will you give your responsibilities the adequate time, effort, and focus that they require without recharging your mental and physical capacities?

Now that you read this chapter, you know what to expect during your first year of college. You have insight into the challenges you might face and the common mistakes you might fall into. Move on to the next chapter to learn about the unique challenges that college courses present and how to prepare for them with ease.

Chapter 2: Study Smarts: Ace Your Classes without Losing Your Mind

Transitioning from high school to college marks a thrilling yet challenging phase in your academic journey. It's a huge shift from the structured environment of high school to the more dynamic setting of college courses. The biggest difference in your school and college life will be the increased academic rigor that comes with college courses. Unlike high school, where the curriculum is more guided, college demands a deeper level of critical thinking, improved analytical skills, and a greater emphasis on independent learning. Your professors expect you to take the initiative in your studies and encourage you to develop a more self-driven approach to learning.

Develop strong organizational skills and the ability to consistently meet deadlines while balancing coursework, extracurricular activities, and personal commitments.

https://www.pexels.com/photo/woman-in-white-long-sleeve-shirt-carrying-a-stack-of-books-4855549/

You will be making your own decisions in your college years. While the autonomy granted by college life gives you the freedom to handle stuff on your terms, it's also necessary to have a heightened sense of responsibility. You'll need to manage your time effectively, make informed decisions about your schedule, and prioritize assignments without the constant supervision or extra coaching you can find in high school. Diverse learning styles are another aspect you'll encounter in college courses. From traditional lectures to group discussions, seminars, and hands-on projects, adapting to this variety demands flexibility and a willingness to engage with the material in ways that may differ from the more standardized methods encountered in high school.

A heavier workload and the need for effective time management add to the challenges. With increased assignments, research projects, and exams, you'll need to develop strong organizational skills and the ability to consistently meet deadlines while balancing coursework, extracurricular activities, and personal commitments. As the courses you opt for will allow you to explore your chosen major in greater depth, this shift will require a higher level of dedication and passion for your chosen subjects compared to the easier curriculum taught in high school classes.

Assessment methods in college also differ significantly, with a greater emphasis on detailed exams, working on projects, and even writing research papers that demand critical analysis. College is more about understanding and applying the concepts in your studies rather than memorization.

As the pressure of studies will increase in your college life, balancing social life and academics is another challenge you have to navigate. While college offers a vibrant social scene, finding the right equilibrium between socializing and academic commitments is crucial.

In facing these challenges, it's essential to cultivate resilience, adaptability, and a proactive approach to your academic journey. However, if you are still feeling overwhelmed due to this transition, share with your parents or consider contacting resources like academic support services and counseling for a successful transition and academic adaptation to the college environment. Your ability to embrace opportunities for growth will lead to a fulfilling and enriching experience during your time in college.

Effective Study Techniques

Crafting a Realistic Study Schedule

After you have settled into your new college routine, you first need to conduct a thorough self-assessment of your daily rhythms and energy patterns. Identify your peak productivity hours, which may vary from person to person. These hours are when you feel most alert and focused. Once you've pinpointed these periods, construct a study schedule that aligns with them. Prioritize challenging tasks during these peak times to capitalize on your heightened cognitive abilities. For example, you can use the peak time to memorize crucial information or use it for critical thinking.

However, it's crucial to inject a dose of realism into your schedule. Recognize that breaks are not only acceptable but essential for maintaining sustained focus. Allocate time for short breaks, allowing your mind to recharge. These intervals will prevent burnout and let you make the most out of your study time.

The Pomodoro Technique

Besides creating a schedule, you can use various time management techniques, like the Pomodoro technique. This technique can significantly enhance your productivity. It involves breaking down your work into intervals, traditionally 25 minutes in length, separated by short breaks. These intervals are referred to as "Pomodoros." After completing four Pomodoros, take a more extended break of 15 to 30 minutes.

This technique operates on the principle of maintaining focus during the designated work interval, knowing that a break is imminent. The structured intervals create a sense of urgency, prevent procrastination, and foster a heightened level of concentration. When implemented correctly, this technique can be a game-changer in optimizing your study sessions.

Note-Taking Optimization

Note-taking is a fundamental aspect of effective studying. Experiment with various methods to find the one that resonates best with your learning style and the nature of the material. Traditional methods, like linear note-taking or the Cornell system, may work well for some, while others might prefer more visual approaches, such as mind maps or concept maps.

Consider the subject matter when choosing your note-taking method. The sciences might benefit from diagrams and charts, while the simple subjects might require detailed textual notes. Don't forget to regularly revisit and revise your notes to increase your understanding and retain them for longer periods.

Active Learning Techniques

Active learning is a pedagogical approach that shifts from passive absorption to active engagement with the material. Techniques such as group discussions, teaching concepts to others, or creating flashcards are effective ways to increase active learning.

Engaging in discussions with peers allows you to view topics from different perspectives, challenging and broadening your understanding. Teaching the material to someone else trains your brain to articulate complex concepts, solidifying your comprehension. Flashcards, particularly in a question-and-answer format, encourage retrieval practice, enhancing both short-term understanding and long-term retention.

Leveraging Technology Wisely

In the digital age, technology can be a valuable ally in your academics. Various applications and tools are available to enhance productivity and organization. Examples include note-taking applications like Evernote or OneNote and task management tools like Todoist or Trello, which can help you organize and prioritize assignments.

However, it's crucial to strike a balance between leveraging technology and avoiding its pitfalls. While apps can enhance efficiency, be mindful of potential distractions and set clear boundaries to use technology as a tool and not a hindrance.

Collaborative Learning

In collaborative learning, you work with peers to achieve common academic goals. This approach taps into the collective knowledge and perspectives of a group, creating a more dynamic and engaging study environment.

Participating in study groups or collaborative projects introduces you to different viewpoints and alternative ways of approaching problems. Engaging in group discussions not only solidifies your understanding but also allows you to learn from your peers. The collaborative exchange of ideas can be particularly beneficial when grappling with complex or challenging subjects.

Retrieval Practice

Retrieval practice is a powerful learning strategy where you actively recall information from memory. This method goes beyond passive reading or reviewing and requires you to actively retrieve information.

You can use these retrieval practices in various forms; you can create flashcards with questions on one side and answers on the other. Quiz yourself on key concepts or write concise summaries from memory. Recalling information strengthens neural connections, promoting better retention and understanding of the material. Use these retrieval practices in your study routine to gradually improve your long-term learning outcomes.

Prioritizing Self-Care

The relationship between well-being and academic performance is symbiotic. Recognizing the importance of self-care is not a luxury but a fundamental necessity for maintaining a healthy mind and body. Prioritize sufficient sleep, regular exercise, and moments of downtime within your schedule.

Getting adequate sleep is essential for cognitive functioning, memory consolidation, and overall well-being. Regular exercise has been linked to improved focus, mood, and stress reduction. Likewise, downtime allows your mind to rest and recharge, preventing burnout and promoting a more balanced and sustainable approach to your studies.

Chunking

It's an excellent strategy where you break down large amounts of information into smaller, manageable units. Instead of attempting to memorize a lengthy passage, divide it into sections or themes. This technique leverages the brain's capacity to process information more efficiently, enhancing both comprehension and retention.

The Eisenhower Matrix

Prioritize tasks using the Eisenhower Matrix, which categorizes activities into four quadrants based on urgency and importance. Using this method, you can identify and focus on high-priority tasks while minimizing time spent on less critical activities.

The Two-Minute Rule

If a task takes two minutes or less to complete, tackle it immediately. This rule helps prevent small tasks from accumulating and becoming overwhelming. Addressing quick tasks promptly will make you more organized and improve the workflow.

Visualization Techniques

In Visualization, you will create mental images of concepts or processes. This technique is particularly beneficial for subjects that involve spatial relationships or complex structures. Visualizing information can enhance understanding and make it easier to recall during exams.

The Feynman Technique

Named after physicist Richard Feynman, this technique involves teaching a concept to someone else as if you were explaining it to a beginner. Simplifying complex ideas and articulating them in straightforward terms increases your understanding of the topic, technique, or concept and identifies gaps in your knowledge.

Time Blocking

Allocate specific blocks of time to different tasks or activities. This method makes it easier to focus on a single task during a designated time period, enhancing concentration and preventing multitasking.

The 80/20 Rule (the Pareto Principle)

The Pareto Principle suggests that roughly 80% of results come from 20% of efforts. Identify the most impactful tasks and concentrate your efforts on them. Recognizing and prioritizing high-impact activities improves your overall efficiency. However, it is necessary to first identify the most important areas of focus and then work on them for the best results.

For example, you can answer around 80% of your exam questions from a subject if you focus on just 20% of the most important material of the subject. This means that a significant portion of your academic success is directly tied to a small fraction of the topics you've covered. However, this principle should never be taken for granted as various subjects require gaining a detailed understanding of the *entire subject.*

Here is an example for more clarity. Say you're preparing for the final exam in a biology course. Upon reviewing your past exam and quiz scores, you realize that the majority of questions focus on a select few key concepts or chapters from the textbook. While you've studied the entire syllabus, you notice that mastering these core topics significantly boosts your overall score.

Consequently, you decide to prioritize your study time accordingly. You dedicate the majority of your study sessions to thoroughly understanding and reviewing the key concepts that are most likely to appear on the exam. This focused approach allows you to maximize your learning efficiency and ensures that you are well-prepared for the most critical aspects of the exam.

By leveraging the 80/20 rule, you can optimize your study efforts, ultimately achieving better academic performance with less time and effort spent overall.

Adaptive Planning

Acknowledge that plans may need to be adjusted due to unforeseen circumstances. Be flexible and adaptive in your approach to study schedules and time management. Developing resilience and the ability to recalibrate when necessary is key to navigating the dynamic nature of college life.

Interleaved Practice

If the topics you need to cover for an exam are related, interleaved practice is a method where you mix different topics or subjects during a study session rather than focusing on a single topic. This technique enhances your ability to discriminate between concepts.

Active Reflection

Regularly evaluate your study methods, time management strategies, and academic progress. Identify what works well and what can be improved. It refines your approach continuously and makes it easier to adapt to the evolving demands of your coursework and academic pursuits.

The nuances of effective study techniques and time management strategies require a tailored and adaptive approach. Experiment with these detailed strategies, continuously refine your methods based on personal preferences and subject requirements – and remain open to new techniques as you navigate the dynamic landscape of college academics.

Campus Resources to Utilize

Besides working on self-care, following a schedule, and incorporating study strategies, effectively utilizing campus resources can be your key to academic success in college. Knowing how to access and utilize support services like extra tutoring classes, study groups, and meeting teachers during office hours can greatly enhance your learning experience. Here's how to make the most of these valuable resources:

Tutoring Classes

Tutoring classes provide either one-on-one or group sessions with experienced tutors who can help clarify challenging concepts, review assignments, and guide you to better understand concepts.

How to utilize them effectively:

Regular attendance: Attend these tutoring sessions consistently, even when you don't have an immediate question. Regular attendance allows tutors to better understand your learning style and tailor their assistance accordingly.

Come Prepared: If possible, bring specific questions or topics you'd like to cover during the session. Prepare in advance to make the most efficient use of your time with the tutor.

While some colleges organize extra classes for students, many institutions may not be available. Another way is to get tutoring assistance from online resources provided by the college.

Study Groups

Study groups are a great way to collaborate with peers, share knowledge, and reinforce your understanding of course materials through discussion and active engagement.

Here are some tips for using study groups effectively:

Diverse Participation: While studying with your friends or peers may seem more comfortable, try engaging with peers from diverse backgrounds and perspectives. This can provide you with alternative viewpoints and strategies for approaching coursework.

Establish Goals: Set clear goals for study group sessions. Whether it's reviewing specific chapters, working on assignments, or preparing for exams, having a purpose will keep the group focused and productive.

Rotate Roles: Assign different roles within the group, such as a discussion leader, a note-taker, and a timekeeper. Rotating roles ensures everyone contributes and benefits from the collaborative effort.

Office Hours

Professors hold office hours – dedicated times when students can meet with them individually or in small groups to discuss course material, seek clarification, or receive additional guidance.

How to utilize them effectively:

Be Proactive: Attend office hours early in the semester, even if you don't have specific questions. Establishing a connection with your professors demonstrates your commitment to the course.

Prepare Questions: If you have questions, come to office hours prepared with specific questions or topics you'd like to discuss.

Seek Clarification: If you're struggling with a concept or assignment, don't hesitate to seek clarification during office hours. Professors are there to help you succeed and are often more than willing to provide additional explanations.

Writing Centers

Writing centers provide assistance with various aspects of the writing process, including brainstorming, outlining, drafting, and revising papers.

How to utilize them effectively:

Start Early: Seek assistance from the writing center early in the writing process. This allows for more comprehensive feedback and improvements.

Have Specific Goals: Clearly communicate your writing goals and any specific area where you're seeking help. This ensures that the writing center staff can provide targeted assistance.

Academic Advising

Schedule regular meetings with your academic advisor to discuss your academic progress, goals, and any challenges you may be facing.
https://www.pexels.com/photo/multiethnic-students-doing-homework-together-in-library-5940716/

What They Offer: Academic advisors can help you plan your course schedule, select a major, and navigate academic requirements.

How to utilize them effectively:

Regular Check-ins: Schedule regular meetings with your academic advisor to discuss your academic progress, goals, and any challenges you may be facing.

Utilize Their Expertise: Advisors can provide insights into potential career paths, internships, and extracurricular activities. Tap into their expertise to make informed decisions about your academic journey.

Campus resources are abundant, and utilizing them effectively is crucial for academic success. Take the initiative to explore these services early on, establish a consistent routine, and approach them with a proactive mindset. Remember, seeking support is a sign of strength and determination, and these resources are designed to help you thrive in your college journey.

Balancing Academics with College Life

As you live your college life, it's crucial to strike a balance between your studies and other aspects. Balancing academics with extracurricular activities, social engagements, and perhaps part-time jobs is essential for a well-rounded and fulfilling college experience. Here's a comprehensive guide on how to prioritize and manage your time effectively while maintaining a healthy and balanced lifestyle:

Prioritize and Set Realistic Goals

Identify Priorities: Clearly outline your academic and personal priorities. Understand the importance of your coursework while acknowledging the value of extracurriculars, social interactions, and any other activity that requires your time.

Set Realistic Goals: Establish achievable short-term and long-term goals. This could include academic objectives, participation in specific activities, or personal development milestones.

Create a Time Management Plan

Use a Planner or Calendar: Utilize a planner or digital calendar to organize your schedule. Include class times, study sessions, extracurricular commitments, and social events.

Block Scheduling: Consider using block scheduling, where specific blocks of time are dedicated to different tasks or types of activities. This approach helps maintain focus and prevent multitasking.

Understand the Impact of Extracurriculars

Enhance Time Management Skills: Engaging in extracurricular activities can develop valuable time management skills. However, be mindful not to overcommit. Prioritize quality over quantity, selecting activities that align with your interests and goals.

Explore Various Interests: While academics are crucial, extracurriculars contribute to personal growth, skill development, and a well-rounded college experience. Explore a variety of interests to discover your passions and develop a diverse skill set.

Social Engagements and Networking

Quality Over Quantity: Balance social engagements with your academic commitments. Prioritize meaningful connections and friendships over a hectic social calendar. Quality interactions contribute to a supportive social network that enhances your overall well-being.

Networking Opportunities: Social engagements provide networking opportunities that can be beneficial to both your personal and professional life. Attend events, join clubs, and participate in activities that align with your interests and career aspirations.

Part-Time Jobs and Academic Performance

Evaluate Time Commitment: If considering part-time employment, assess the time commitment required and how it aligns with your academic responsibilities. Choose positions that offer flexibility and consider the potential impact on your studies.

Communicate with Employers: Clearly communicate your academic commitments with your employer. Many employers in college towns understand the academic demands placed on students and are often willing to accommodate reasonable requests.

Tips for Maintaining a Healthy Balance

Practice Self-Care: Prioritize self-care by getting adequate sleep, engaging in regular physical activity, and maintaining a balanced diet. Taking care of your physical and mental well-being is crucial for sustaining a busy college lifestyle.

Learn to Say No: Recognize your limits and be comfortable saying no when necessary. It's okay to decline additional commitments if they jeopardize your well-being or academic performance.

Reflect Regularly: Periodically reflect on your commitments and reassess your priorities. College is a dynamic experience, and your goals and interests may evolve over time.

Balancing academics with other aspects of college life requires intentionality, self-awareness, and effective time management. Embrace the opportunities for personal and academic growth, recognizing that your college experience can pave the way to long-term success and fulfillment.

Chapter 3: Dorm Room Diplomacy: Living in Harmony with Roommates

As you're getting ready for independence, it's time to think about dorm life. While you're excited to jazz up your dorm room and hang out with your new pals for late-night burgers, there's something really important to consider: your roommate. They can totally shape how your college life goes, for better or for worse. This one crucial detail about college has the power to make or break your college experience.

Yes, that person you'll be sharing a slightly bigger than a shoebox-sized space with, whose sleep schedule might be the complete opposite of yours, and whose taste in music could be, well... let's just say, "unique." But fear not. Don't worry about your 'roommate' situation. It won't be a total nightmare. This chapter will help you turn your dorm room into a peaceful, calm, and productive space. Imagine studying late with your roommate, laughing, and sharing snacks instead of fighting over who has what and what goes where. Sounds great, right? Well, it can be your reality.

Not having clear communication can hinder any kind of relationship.
https://www.pexels.com/photo/woman-in-white-shirt-and-yellow-shorts-standing-beside-bed-4004131/

Turning that random roommate assignment into a potential friendship (or, at the very least, a peaceful coexistence) is doable. Your experience doesn't have to correspond with horror stories about messy habits and territorial battles during college; with the correct mindset and the right approach, you can cultivate an atmosphere of peace within your living environment and push roommate rivalries outside the door until they go in search of shelter somewhere else.

In this chapter, you'll learn how to handle roommate situations calmly and find solutions peacefully, understand the common fears and concerns of having a roommate, and explore the possibility of having your roommate as an ally and the rewarding aspects that come with it. It doesn't matter if you're a social butterfly who thrives on company or a quiet studier who prefers peace and quiet – you'll learn a lot from this chapter.

Everything from setting clear boundaries to navigating inevitable personality clashes and building good communication skills will be tackled here. Clear communication is the secret ingredient to cooking any successful relationship, even the roommate kind. By the end of this chapter, you'll be a dorm room diplomat extraordinaire, ready to conquer college life with confidence and a smile, and maybe a pair of noise-canceling headphones – just in case. Those come in handy most of the time.

Moving from Stranger to Roommate

It's natural to feel apprehensive about living with someone new. Sharing your space with a stranger can feel like a coin toss. Will you end up with your own personal gaming buddy or someone who leaves dirty dishes piled high and blasts heavy metal at 3 AM? You never know until you meet them. The journey from stranger to roommate can be exciting and sometimes awkward. But it's college, so you have to be ready for anything.

Understanding Common Concerns and Fears

Living with a stranger can bring up all sorts of worries and uncertainties. You might be concerned about not getting along, invading each other's privacy, or sharing belongings. These concerns are entirely normal and shared by many freshmen embarking on this new journey. You need to acknowledge and understand these common concerns to better prepare yourself for the challenges ahead and take proactive steps to address them. The common fears include:

- Fear of the unknown.
- Worries about compatibility.
- Concerns about personal space.

Building Rapport from Day One

To ensure a positive roommate experience, you need to lay the groundwork for a strong relationship right from the start. This means making an effort to get to know your roommate, being open and friendly, and showing respect for each other's space and boundaries. Here are strategies to help you with that:

1. **Break the ice.** Once you have your roommate assignment, you can reach out via email or social media to introduce yourself. If you have to meet them in person, that's even better. Share your name, and share a little something interesting about yourself. Maybe you collect vintage comic books, can juggle three balls, or bake the best chocolate chip cookies you have ever tasted! (You can also throw in a friendly handshake with a smile . . .)

2. **Get to know each other.** Ask them questions about themselves. What are their hobbies? Favorite movies? Why did they choose the college? Don't be shy about sharing your own interests, too. This will help you find common ground and build a connection with your roommate.
3. **Ask for help.** You don't need to do everything by yourself. You can show your roommate you are open to collaboration when you ask for help. Ask your new roommate if they'd be up for lending a hand (or a muscle) when you need one, and ask them for their recommendations sometimes. Even if it's just carrying a few boxes, it shows you appreciate their support.
4. **Give small gifts.** Maybe you wouldn't bring a giant bouquet of flowers on day one, but a small gift can show you care and make a positive impression. It doesn't have to be expensive - thoughtfulness is what counts. It can spark a conversation and create a friendly atmosphere.
5. **Be flexible.** Understand that living with someone new might mean small or big changes. Be ready to adjust and give in on some things to keep a happy and peaceful living space.

The Place of Respect and Boundaries

Living with someone, especially for the first time, can be like baking a cake together - some may enjoy rich chocolate layers, while others prefer a lighter vanilla sponge. The key to enjoying the cake (and your dorm life) is understanding everyone's preferences and making sure everyone gets a cut. This translates to respect and boundaries when it comes to cohabiting with a college roommate. They are the building blocks of a happy and stress-free living space. To establish mutual respect and boundaries, do the following:

Define Your Needs: Before diving into setting boundaries, take some time to figure out what you need to feel comfortable and respected in your dorm room. Think about things like:

a. What is your sleep schedule like? Are you an early bird or a night owl? Do you need complete silence to fall asleep, or can you handle some background noise?
b. Are you a neat freak? How tidy do you like to keep things? Are you okay with a few crumbs on the desk, or do you prefer a spotless environment?
c. What are your study habits? Do you need complete quiet to focus, or do you enjoy studying with some background music or the TV on?
d. What about other people? How comfortable are you with your roommate having friends over? Is there a limit on the number of people or how late they can stay?

Once you've identified your needs, don't bottle them up or swallow them. You will choke at some point. More importantly, understand that you didn't come to college for a mind-reading competition. Your roommate cannot peek into your mind to tell what your needs are unless you tell them. Try these to communicate your needs clearly:

1. Practice using "I" statements more often. So, instead of accusing your roommate of being messy, say something like, "I feel more comfortable studying when the desk is clear."
2. Don't beat around the bush - be specific. Don't just say you need quiet - explain what kind of quiet you need. "I can focus with some background noise, but loud music or people talking makes it hard for me to concentrate."
3. Stay open-minded. You're not the only one with needs. Your roommate has needs, too. So, be prepared to hear their perspective and find compromises.

Establish Clear Boundaries: Boundaries are essentially the lines you draw to create a comfortable and respectful living environment. Think of them like invisible walls that separate your "space" from your roommate's. To establish clear boundaries with your roommate:

a. **Have a "Roommate Agreement":** This doesn't have to be a formal contract, but it's a great way to discuss and document your expectations. Talk about things like quiet hours, guest policies, cleaning schedules, and how you'll handle shared items like the fridge or TV.

b. **Respect Their Personal Space:** Just because you share a room doesn't mean you have to be on top of each other all the time. Respect each other's need for privacy, especially during study sessions or when relaxing.

c. **Tell Them about Any Changes:** Life happens, and sometimes you might need to adjust your boundaries. Maybe you have a big exam coming up and need complete silence for a few days. Let your roommate know beforehand and be understanding if they need the same kind of accommodation sometimes.

d. **Be Willing to Compromise:** There will be times when your needs and wants clash. Instead of digging your heels in, find a middle ground. You could agree to alternate nights for having guests or designate specific areas of the room for each of your belongings.

Boundaries and respect go both ways. Be willing to give what you expect. The more you practice having clear conversations about your needs and respecting the needs of your roommate, the more your dorm room will feel like a home, not a battleground.

Effective Communication and Conflict Resolution

Living with someone is bound to lead to disagreements, just like ketchup inevitably ends up on some people's fries, even though they have no business together. The good news is that effective communication and conflict-resolution skills can turn those disagreements into minor bumps in the road, not roadblocks.

The Art of Active Listening

A big part of communication is truly listening to your roommate. You shouldn't be zoning out while they talk. Active listening means paying attention to what they're saying and trying to understand their perspective. Here are some tips to become better at actively listening to your roommate:

- Put away your phone, turn off the TV, and make eye contact with your roommate. Give them your full attention.
- Make use of your body language. Nod your head, lean in slightly, and avoid crossing your arms. This shows you're engaged and interested.
- Ask clarifying questions before you jump to conclusions. Make sure you understand their point of view before responding.
- Summarize what you heard and briefly repeat what your roommate said to show you were paying attention.

Step-by-Step Guide to Addressing Issues Constructively

Say your roommate left dirty dishes piled high in the sink again. Here's a step-by-step approach to address the issue constructively:

Step 1: Pick the right place and time. Don't try to have a serious conversation when you're both stressed and tired. Wait for a calm moment when you can talk things through without emotions running high.

Step 2: Start with "I" statements. Instead of accusing your roommate of being a slob, try something like, "I feel frustrated when the dishes pile up because it makes the kitchen feel messy." This helps focus on the issue and avoids putting your roommate on the defensive.

Step 3: It's no use playing the blame game. Instead, point out the problem and suggest ways to fix it. For example, you could propose a chore chart or agree to take turns cleaning up after meals.

Step 4: Compromise when necessary. You never know – there might be a good reason for the dirty dishes. Maybe your roommate has a busy schedule. Be willing to find a solution that works for both of you.

Step 5: End on a positive note. Even if you don't reach a complete agreement right away, acknowledge the effort to talk things through. End the conversation with a positive tone and a willingness to revisit it later if needed.

Step 6: Don't forget that this is a conversation, not a confrontation. The goal is to find a solution that works for both of you – not to win an argument.

Real-life Scenarios: Putting communication skills into practice

Scenario 1:
Your roommate has friends over every night, and the dorm room feels more like a party zone than a study space.

What do you do?
- Talk to your roommate about setting clear guest policies.
- Agree on a reasonable number of guests allowed at a time.
- Set a curfew for weekdays.

Scenario 2:
Your roommate studies late with the lights on, while you need complete darkness to sleep.

What do you do?
- Invest in an eye mask for yourself.
- You can get a small desk lamp for your roommate as a gift.
- Talk about quiet hours when lights need to be out, even if someone is still awake studying.

The Perks of Having a Roommate

Sure, sharing a dorm room comes with its challenges. But the truth is, having a roommate can be pretty great, too. Beyond just cohabitating, a good roommate can become a friend, a confidante, and even a partner in crime (the good kind, of course). Here are some of the unexpected perks of having a roommate:

College is an adventure – a whirlwind of new experiences, challenges, and a lot of fun. And, while you might be picturing yourself exploring the campus with a squad of newfound friends, the truth is, your roommate might be your first and probably closest college companion. Sure, they're the person you share a desk lamp with, but they also have the potential to become a valuable ally on your college journey.

You go from roommates to allies. In your freshman-year dorm room, your interactions with your roommate might be limited to polite hellos and the occasional awkward silence. But here's the thing: that blank canvas has the potential to become a masterpiece of friendship. Having a roommate can blossom into something more.

You get a built-in support system. College can be tough. There will be times when you're feeling overwhelmed, stressed, or homesick. Having a roommate who understands what you're going through can be a huge source of comfort and support.

You have shared experiences. From late-night study sessions fueled by questionable snacks to celebrating good grades and surviving finals week together, you'll share a unique set of experiences with your roommate. These shared moments can create a strong bond.

You learn from each other. We all come from different backgrounds and have different perspectives. Living with someone who might not see the world exactly like you do can be a great way to learn and grow. Embrace your differences and be open to seeing things from their point of view.

Collaboration through Décor

Having a roommate means you get to double the decorating power!
https://www.pexels.com/photo/two-girls-decorating-a-christmas-tree-5618029/

Your dorm room isn't just a place to sleep; it's your home away from home. Having a roommate means you get to double the decorating power! Pool your resources and brainstorm ideas to turn your bland dorm room into a space that reflects both of your personalities.

Mix and Match Styles: Maybe you love cool lights and throw pillows, while your roommate prefers a minimalist look. Look for the common ground and combine some of your favorite elements to create a unique and stylish space.

DIY Projects: Dorm rooms are notorious for being small. You and your roommate can work together on some DIY projects, like building shelves for extra storage or creating a cozy reading nook in a corner.

Get Creative on a Budget: Dorm decorating doesn't have to break the bank. You can visit thrift stores for vintage finds or get crafty with some colorful throw pillows made from old t-shirts.

Organizing Shared Responsibilities

To be honest, keeping a dorm room clean and organized can feel like a full-time job, especially during a quiz week. Having a roommate means you can share the responsibilities, making things a whole lot easier. To do this effectively:

1. Sit down with your roommate and create a weekly or monthly chore chart. This way, you both know what needs to be done and who's responsible for what.
2. Split the costs into equal parts. Sharing groceries, cleaning supplies, or even streaming services can save you both some money. Talk about what makes sense to split and come up with a system that works for both of you.
3. Be flexible and understanding. Life happens, and sometimes, one of you might be swamped with work or exams. Be flexible and willing to pick up the slack for your roommate when they need it. They'll do the same for you in return.

Building Memories Together

Having a roommate can turn everyday college life into a series of fun and unforgettable memories. You'll be each other's built-in study buddies, movie marathon partners, and even emergency snack suppliers (we've all been there!). Here are some things you can do together:

1. Try new restaurants, attend campus events, or discover hidden spots on campus. Having a roommate makes everything more fun and adventurous.
2. Errands can be adventures. Going grocery shopping or just cleaning the room doesn't have to be a chore. Turn it into a fun time with your roommate. Turn up the music, try a new recipe together, and make even the most mundane tasks shared experiences.
3. You can become friends or more. Living with someone can be a great way to build strong friendships. You'll share secrets, celebrate victories, and offer support during tough times.

Navigating Differences and Finding Common Ground

Not every roommate situation is going to be sunshine and rainbows, and that's a fact. But these differences don't have to be dealbreakers. Here are some tips for navigating differences and finding common ground with your roommate:

- Have an honest conversation about the issue. Don't be afraid to voice your concerns, but do so respectfully.
- Meet each other halfway. It's allowed. Make room for their needs, too.
- Even if you don't see eye-to-eye on everything, there are bound to be some things you have in common. Share activities you both enjoy - it'll help strengthen your bond and create positive memories.

Finally, dear college star, understand that friendship isn't always instant. It takes time, effort, and a willingness to put yourself out there. Don't be afraid to initiate conversations, invite your roommate to join you for activities, or simply have dinner together and chat about your day. Living with a roommate is a learning experience. It can teach you valuable skills like communication, compromise, and respect. Embracing your differences and finding common ground can turn your roommate from a cohabitant into a true friend and a valuable ally on your college journey.

Chapter 4: Navigating Nutrition on Campus

College students have several options when it comes to satisfying their nutritional needs. Those who live on campus often eat at a cafeteria on campus, getting their meals through the meal plans they buy at the beginning of the semester. Depending on the size and location of the college, meal plans can include a variety of cuisines, niche foods, and even the option to expand your plan for buying snacks, coffee, or other beverages.

Some students prefer not to eat in the cafeteria but in the dorm room or, if they live off campus, in their apartment. Besides the on-campus cafeteria-style lunch counter you'll find at most colleges, students have plenty of other brick-and-mortar and mobile restaurants (food trucks) on and near the campus at their disposal.

Students eat on the go between classes and study sessions, so they're looking for something quick to grab.
https://www.pexels.com/photo/man-eating-pizza-and-working-from-home-4841733/

Whichever option you prefer, rest assured that you'll find plenty of variety to avoid boring meals. However, all these choices can be overwhelming, especially if you want to have a balanced diet. After all, the most represented option in all restaurants will be fast food - given that lots of students eat on the go between classes and study sessions, so they're looking for something quick to grab.

The good news? This chapter will guide you through the process of making healthy nutritional choices, emphasizing the importance of eating nutritionally balanced meals, including maintaining energy, focus, and overall health in the challenging college setting. You'll receive plenty of tips on navigating your nutritional choices on campus and using mealtime to relax and socialize with fellow students.

The Importance of Nutrition for Students

Sometimes, when trying to juggle school obligations, social life, and more, the last thing on your mind will probably be nutrition. You eat when you can, grab what you can gulp down the fastest, and don't think of it anymore. This is how many college students think and live - not realizing that making healthier nutritional choices could help them balance their tasks more effectively. The right food can be fuel that gets you through challenging times, and here is why.

It's Better for Your Physical Health

You probably have heard it before, but eating nutrient-rich meals is better for your health. Your muscles use energy, which comes from carbs and fats. At the same time, your muscles are built of proteins. Whenever you're physically active, your muscles use the energy to move your body. While they do, they break down a little bit, so they have to rebuild themselves. By eating meals and snacks that contain all the food groups throughout the day, you fuel your muscles with adequate resources.

Your body also needs vitamins and minerals, which you get from a variety of food choices. These will help you prevent illnesses (like the nasty flu you get when you're supposed to be studying or, even worse, enjoying a free night with your friends). Hassling through a demanding schedule can be draining and easily deplete your body of essential nutrients, which is why it's crucial to replenish them through balanced meals.

It Boosts Academic Performance

Besides nourishing your body, nutrient-rich foods can also fuel your mind. You see, the muscles aren't the only ones using energy in your body. Your brain needs plenty of fuel, too. Moreover, it requires a constant supply of energy. Fast and sugary food only provides a quick burst of energy, which then drops, leaving you sluggish and unable to focus. By contrast, a more balanced diet will help you concentrate on your lessons and study sessions, process and memorize the information you've learned, and obtain higher grades. Fruit and vegetables are also full of antioxidants, which boost blood flow, enabling your body to supply plenty of energy to your brain.

It Will Put You in a Better Mood

College life can be overwhelming, and sometimes you won't feel like doing anything. Maybe you'll feel like you could have done better on an exam or assignment, or maybe you'll feel as if juggling all your obligations and pressing deadlines is becoming a little too much to handle. Whenever something dampens your mood, food can come to the rescue and make you feel better about yourself. Your mood depends on your brain chemistry, or more precisely, whichever hormone is being released in your brain. Dopamine and serotonin are the two famous feel-good hormones, and you would be surprised how easy it is to boost their production with the help of the right foods. For example, fish are high in Omega 3 fatty acids, which will make the brain produce more dopamine and chase away your depression. Eating fermented food like sauerkraut, kimchi, or yogurt is a wonderful way to boost your serotonin level. Serotonin is responsible for keeping your mood up longer – and do you know what else can help you maintain its production? Chocolate. Dark chocolate (made from a major part of cocoa butter and cocoa powder) is also great for improving blood flow to the brain.

It Supports Weight Management

Maintaining a healthy weight goes beyond aesthetic appearance. It's the key to preventing illnesses and improving your productivity. College is a time for extreme changes, including switching to a slightly more sedentary lifestyle, study schedules, lack of sleep, and more. All these can increase your stress levels, which will take a toll on your metabolism and cause your weight to fluctuate.

It Helps You Sleep Better

Besides worrying about how you'll perform on the next exam or juggling all your studies, work, and social obligations, eating unhealthy food can also make you lose sleep. Skipping meals and eating nutrient-dense food at night makes it harder to digest your meals. Your metabolism slows down when you skip breakfast and have a quick, light lunch. So, when you overload it with high-fat food at night (because, by this time, you feel like you're starving), your body is too busy digesting to let you sleep. Eating several balanced meals throughout the day will continually supply you with nutrients your body can digest and access much easier, and as a result, you'll sleep better and longer.

How to Navigate Your Nutrition Choices

Now that you know the benefits of making healthier food choices, it's time to learn how to navigate them.

Don't Skip Breakfast

It may be tempting to skip breakfast (especially if you wake up late), but avoid this whenever possible. Besides slowing your metabolism, skipping breakfast leaves your brain without fuel right at the start of your day. This is like going on a long drive without hardly any fuel in your tank. To avoid running on empty, have at least some protein and fruits for breakfast. In the cafeteria, opt for something like a breakfast bar or loaded toast.

Try to avoid eating sugary foods for breakfast regularly. A bowl of cereal or pancakes is okay now and then, but these won't keep you full for long, so protein sources are always a better option for breakfast. You can always add some whole-grain toast for some fiber, too, to your protein-rich breakfast.

If you are running late, grab a granola bar (preferably with nuts in it for added protein intake). An even better option would be to prepare your breakfast the night before so you don't have to worry about making it in the morning. For example, overnight oats are an easy-to-prepare yet filling option you can make on campus.

Here is an overnight oat recipe for you to try.

Ingredients:

- 1/2 cup of rolled oats or quick oats
- 1/2 cup of your favorite milk

- 1 to 2 tablespoons of chia seeds
- 1 teaspoon of honey or natural sweetener like maple syrup or agave nectar
- seasonal fruit

Instructions:

1. Before going to bed, mix all ingredients in a sealable jar or bowl – except the fruit. If you're using fruit like bananas, you can add them if you wish.
2. Put the mixture in the fridge, and top it off with fruit in the morning.

Weigh In Your Options at the Cafeteria

The college cafeteria is a convenient option for students living on campus, but it often has plenty of unhealthy options. Whenever possible, skip overly-processed meals, which mainly contain sugar. Whole grains are a better source of carbs that will keep you full longer. Likewise, grilled meat is a better source of protein than fried meat because it fills up with more protein than unhealthy fats. Pay attention to your salads, too. Some are loaded with unhealthy dressings made of processed ingredients or high in fat and sugar. If your school cafeteria has a salad bar, prepare your salads with healthy dressings – you can never go wrong with olive oil and vinegar.

Be Careful with Sugar

Unfortunately, simple sugars (the ones that spike your blood sugar levels and cause the inevitable crash that follows) are found in almost every type of processed food, even in the savory variety. It's not only the sugary drinks and baked goods you have to worry about. Sugar is often added to salad dressings, soups, sauces, and meat products. When buying ready-made food, make sure to read the nutritional information on the label to avoid taking in too much sugar throughout the day.

Drink Plenty of Water

Water is essential for digestion. If you want your body to use the healthy fuel you're getting through your meals, you'll need to drink eight to 10 cups of water a day. On a hot day, water will keep you hydrated and help you maintain focus. Not only that, but drinking more water will also prevent you from reaching for sugary drinks. A great way to ensure you're staying hydrated is to keep a reusable water bottle with you wherever you go. If you find drinking plain water boring, switch it up with fruit juice or carbonated water occasionally.

Keep To-Go Snacks in Your Bag

There is nothing wrong with having an unhealthy snack from time to time – as long as you're reaching for healthy options the rest of the time. Buy or make healthy snacks you can keep in your bag or room for a to-go or last-minute option. It will save you money and prevent you from giving in to cravings for sugary or processed foods. Nuts and dried fruit are not only convenient to carry but are some of the easiest ways to snack healthy in college.

Be Aware of your Caffeine Intake

On long study sessions and busy days, it will be tempting to fuel your body with loads of caffeine. However, excessive caffeine has a negative effect on your mood, and it won't keep your focus longer, either. If anything, drinking too much of it will make you feel even more exhausted. Limit your caffeine intake to two cups of tea or coffee a day, and avoid energy drinks because these are also high in sugar and harmful processed ingredients. It will make you feel better, and if you need a little pick me up, a handful of healthy snacks will always be a better option.

Plan Your Grocery Shopping

Before you head out to the store for snacks and ingredients to prepare easy meals in your room, *create a grocery list*. Include lots of healthy snacks and food that'll provide your body with the right nutrients, like protein, healthy fats, and complex carbs. Aim to buy enough ingredients that'll last you for a week so you won't be tempted to purchase unhealthy options when you run out of healthy ones.

If you worry that healthy foods will strain your budget, look for student discounts, items on sale, and coupons that'll help you save money on groceries. It's always a good idea to use generic options instead of brand names. Buy only seasonal produce as it is always cheaper, and most importantly, never go to the store or market hungry, as this will make it more tempting for you to choose quick-meal options, which are often ultra-processed and unhealthy.

Give Meal Prepping a Try

Meal planning and prepping can be a lifesaver for those days when you're too busy to go to the cafeteria or cook a healthy meal. Of course, you probably don't have time to prepare all your meals in advance, but prepping even one meal a day will go a long way toward maintaining a healthy diet.

Easy access to pre-made meals will prevent you from unhealthy options like fast food, and it will also save you money. Meal prepping will particularly come in handy when you're busy during the day but still want to eat something healthy for lunch or dinner.

Avoid Late-Night Snacking

Except for all-night study sessions, you should avoid eating anything close to bedtime.
https://www.pexels.com/photo/young-man-eating-snacks-and-watching-tv-9807579/

Remember, the snacks and other treats you keep in your dorm room or apartment are there to keep you away from unhealthy options when you're in a time crunch. They're not there, so you can fill yourself up on them as a late snack after not eating enough during the day. Except for all-night study sessions, you should avoid eating anything close to bedtime. By dispersing your meals evenly throughout the day, you can prevent yourself from falling into the pitfalls of late-night snacking.

Don't Forget to Indulge on Occasion

If there are times when you can't stick to a healthy diet, don't worry. You can reach for an unhealthy snack or meal while on the go – just do it sparingly. If you want to celebrate a big milestone in college life with ice cream and cake, go ahead. Following a strict healthy regime can feel restricting, so indulging in a not-so-healthy option on occasion will help you even out the balance in your diet.

Having fun with food will also help you build a healthy relationship with it. While food is necessary for survival, it should never be an enemy, and eating should never feel like an obligation or coping mechanism. A balanced diet will help you avoid falling into unhealthy eating habits like over- or undereating, stress-eating, and more. You can enjoy everything in moderation as long as you focus on nutritious choices whenever possible.

Establish a Mealtime Routine

Keeping a consistent mealtime routine will help you avoid skipping meals and late-night snacks, and you will stay focused during classes and study sessions. One of the best ways to stick to a routine is to include friends and roommates. Make plans to eat together or help each other out when to-go meals are the only option. It will keep you motivated to fuel your body regularly and socialize with your peers.

Aim for Variety

You may quickly find your favorite healthy food choices at the cafeteria, restaurant, or among the meals you prepare on your own. However, by sticking to the same items all the time, you won't have a balanced diet. For example, eating a salad for dinner is a great option, but doing it every night will make you miss out on other foods like proteins or whole-grain baked goods.

Even if you know which items should be on your plate for a balanced diet, being surrounded by so many choices on the college campus can make it challenging to include variety in your meals. Here are a few ideas on how to achieve this:

- **Portion the Food:** For your main meals, half of your plate should be filled with vegetables and fruits, a quarter with carbs (preferably whole grain), and the last quarter with protein sources. You can also add a side of dairy or a dairy substitute.
- **Include Lots of Colors:** One of the best indications of a healthy diet is seeing lots of colors on your plate. The more colors you have in your meals, the greater the variety of nutrients you're giving your body.
- **Switch up the Veggies:** While salad bars and ready-to-eat packaged salads may seem convenient, there are plenty of other veggies and ways to eat them. For example, in some food trucks, you can create your own wraps by including a range of ingredients – it's a great way to switch up the veggies and try a variety of flavor combinations. In restaurants or if you have a hot bar in the campus cafeteria, try sautéed or cooked veggies.

You can also create quick and interesting salads, like the following nectarine and beet salad, in your dorm room.

Ingredients:
- 2 medium nectarines, sliced
- 2 5-ounce packages of spring mix salad greens
- 1/2 cup of balsamic vinaigrette
- 1/2 cup of crumbled feta cheese
- 1 14-1/2 ounce can have sliced beets

Instructions:
1. In a bowl, mix the nectarines and greens, sprinkling them with vinaigrette.
2. Top with the cheese and beets, and enjoy.

Pay Attention to the Descriptions

When it comes to ready meals or meals you can get from a campus cafeteria or nearby restaurant, the description can tell you a lot about them, like their nutritional value and caloric content. For example, if you see something described as "rich" or "creamy," it's likely high in calories and saturated fat. The same applies to most fried food, while baked, sautéed, or grilled options typically contain less fat and calories.

The food descriptions can also tell you if the meal is suitable for vegans and vegetarians or whether it contains something you're allergic to. Some cafeterias have a separate section clearly labeled *vegan/vegetarian*, just like some restaurant menus do. When in doubt, you can always ask whether something is suitable for your diet based on your needs and potential allergies.

The Implications Of Eating Habits On Student Life

The implications of your eating habits go far beyond your physical and mental health and well-being. Student life can be stressful, so the social expectation of dining can bring you much-needed relief. Whether having one meal together in the campus cafeteria or nearby restaurant or having a quick snack on your study break while catching up with your mate or friends, there can all be opportunities for socializing and relaxation amid your busy schedules.

College is the time when young people are working toward similar goals, so you'll always have a lot to talk about during joint mealtimes. Whether you live on campus or in a nearby apartment, you'll likely eat somewhere nearby, and consuming food with your college friends will become one of your main social activities. Your shared dining experiences will help you forge powerful bonds with your community. There is a good reason why many colleges showcase their cafeteria in the experience programs they advertise for potential students – they know that seeing how they can socialize can be a decisive factor for prospective students.

Chapter 5: Balancing Fun and Studies

Time and again, you may have heard from older kids and graduate seniors that college is more fun than school. So far in the book, it has seemed to be simply an adult version of your school with more independence. It's time to behold the fun side of college and find ways to balance it with your studies.

It's time to behold the fun side of college and find ways to balance it with your studies.
https://www.pexels.com/photo/cheerful-young-lady-in-creative-studio-3876297/

You might have had extracurriculars at school and even participated in a few, but college extracurriculars are a whole different ball game. They are highly competitive, immensely advanced, and infinitely more exciting. Did you know you have a chance to be selected for a national- or international-level sports club or team if you play well in college?

Value of Extracurriculars

Extracurriculars are subjects or activities that supplement academic coursework. You don't have to take them up, but they can prove to be as important as your curriculum.

- **Skill Development:** Extracurricular activities provide opportunities to develop a wide range of skills, such as leadership, teamwork, communication, time management, and problem-solving. You saw their importance in the previous chapter for academic success. They are also highly valued by employers and are essential for personal and professional success.
- **Exploration of Interests:** College is a time for exploration and self-discovery. Extracurriculars help you explore new interests and hobbies outside of your academic studies so you can develop a well-rounded goal for the future. For instance, if your academic passion is physics, you may also like to play in an orchestra. You won't know unless you try. Albert Einstein had a passion for both physics and music!
- **Networking Opportunities:** Participating in extracurriculars helps you connect with peers who share similar interests. It will also give you a chance to interact with faculty, alumni, and professionals in the field. These connections can lead to valuable friendships, mentorships, and even job opportunities in the future.
- **Enhanced Resume:** In a competitive job market, employers look for candidates who demonstrate a well-rounded skill set and a commitment to activities beyond academics. Listing extracurricular involvement on a resume can help you stand out and showcase your diverse talents and interests.
- **Personal Growth:** These provide opportunities for self-improvement. They can boost confidence, foster creativity, and help you develop a sense of identity and purpose outside of your academic achievements.
- **Balanced Lifestyle:** The advanced college coursework can lead to stress. Extracurriculars have the power to destress you after a hard day in classes. Playing a sport you love or doing an activity you adore can prove to be a calming presence in your hectic college life.
- **Leadership Opportunities:** Many activities offer leadership positions, like club president, team captain, or event organizer. These roles allow you to develop leadership skills, take initiative, and make a positive impact within (and even beyond) the campus community.
- **Preparation for the Real World:** Extracurriculars provide college-level insight into the real world. They are like miniature worlds in themselves, where you can get a taste of what's to come. Whether it's leading a team project, organizing an event, or collaborating with diverse groups of people, these experiences will prepare you for the challenges you will face in the future.

Extracurricular Options

Your extracurricular activities may have been limited in school, but in college, they are numerous and diverse, depending on the university.

- **Student Clubs and Organizations:** Almost every U.S. college offers a wide range of student-run clubs and organizations focused on a variety of interests and activities. These can include academic clubs related to specific majors or fields of study (math clubs, film, etc.), cultural and ethnic clubs (music or dance based on different countries), political and social activism groups (political science, debates, etc.), arts and performance organizations (acting clubs), recreational sports clubs (swimming, cycling, etc.), and more.

- **Sports:** Many colleges have varsity sports teams competing at intercollegiate levels. If you want to play in a less competitive environment, go with intramural sports leagues conducted within the university alone. If your college has enough resources, you can play virtually any sport, from soccer and football to chess and snooker.
- **Volunteer and Community Service Programs:** Do you want to help your community instead? You can opt for volunteer work and community service projects that are active in your college. This can include tutoring and mentoring programs, environmental conservation initiatives, outreach to underserved communities, fundraising events, and disaster relief efforts.
- **Student Government:** Do you wish to try out politics before pursuing a career in it? Dip your toes in it through the student government at your college. There are student councils, senates, or class councils where you can represent your peers, advocate for student interests, and organize campus events and initiatives. The leadership experience gained through these organizations will propel your career to newer heights.
- **Arts and Performance Groups:** Arts and performance hold a treasure trove of possibilities, and not all of them are available in the curriculum. To expand your horizons in music, theater, dance, visual arts, and other creative pursuits, join the related group. At times, they may also produce concerts, plays, art exhibitions, dance performances, and other cultural events on campus.
- **Media and Publications:** Are you interested in journalism, filmmaking, or writing? Various media and publications clubs on campus create and manage college newspapers, magazines, radio stations, TV stations, or online publications. With their help, you can acquire several skills, including reporting, editing, production, and storytelling.
- **Religious and Spiritual Organizations:** Dive into your own religion or explore other religions and philosophies through the relevant groups. Many colleges have diverse organizations that provide support, fellowship, and opportunities for worship and religious exploration. These groups may host religious services, discussions, retreats, community service projects, and other social events that promote their cause.

The best part is you can start your own extracurricular activity. Opening an interest-related club is a simple three-stage process:

1. Define the purpose, goals, and values of your club.
2. Ask a faculty member for advice and assistance in developing the club's specifics.
3. Fill up a registration form.

Your extracurriculars can supplement your academic milestones and goals, providing you with the tools to achieve them. They can be as rewarding and exciting as your studies, so much so that you would be hard-pressed to choose between the two. You need to strike a balance between them to experience a fulfilling college life.

Balancing Fun with Academic Obligations

Imagine you are doing something you love, like painting. You may become so engrossed in your art that you forget your other chores. Having lunch or dinner may also slip your mind. Having a passion and indulging in it is great, but you need to keep a set schedule for other tasks to maintain your overall well-being.

Similarly, you can become so passionate about an extracurricular activity that you forget to study the curriculum! How can you manage to spend just the right amount of time studying and having fun?

Effective Time Management

In a bid to discover yourself and establish your identity, you tend to take on a lot of stuff. As you try to get everything done, it increases your stress levels, and you end up doing nothing at all. The solution is to allocate specific times of your day to specific tasks so you can do everything you want to do without letting it affect your health.

- **Create a Timetable:** This is the most basic time-management technique you learned in school, which is equally effective in college.
    1. Write down a list of all the tasks you NEED to complete during the day (studies and extracurriculars).
    2. Write down things you WISH to do (like hanging out with friends).
    3. Estimate the time for each task you need to do and add it to your timetable.
    4. Estimate the time for each thing you wish to do and fill in the gaps in the table.

Make a habit of creating a timetable every Monday morning. Include the time-blocking technique to block every minute of your waking hours for an activity, whether it is studies or relaxation. Use the following table for reference; you can change the hourly intervals to suit your own needs:

	Mon	Tue	Wed	Thurs	Fri	Sat	Sun
8 AM to 9 AM							
8 PM to 9 PM							

- **Use a Planner or a Calendar:** The sheer number of tasks and obligations you have at this age can often become overwhelming. You don't want to find yourself in a situation where you have scheduled your family get-together and school reunion on the same day as your college tests. Planning for the entire month in advance helps a great deal, and noting down the important events throughout the year, like Thanksgiving dinner, avoids getting your schedules mixed up.

Use a planner or a calendar to make a note of those important dates. Don't forget to refer back to it each time you create a daily or weekly timetable. If you don't have a physical calendar, download one on your smartphone or use a planner app like Microsoft Planner.

- **Set Reminders:** Have you created your schedule for the day, week, and month? Good going. All you need to do is keep referring to it from time to time to make sure you're following it. What if you forget to check it out and miss a task? Reminders will help you out.

At the beginning of each day, set a reminder on your phone for each task, no matter how small. Set reminders for breaks and relaxation, too. The incessant rings may become annoying over time, so keep a different tone for each reminder or record inspiring quotes to pump yourself up for the next task.

Useful Time Management Techniques

Incorporate these tried and tested time-management techniques in your schedule to balance fun and studies more efficiently:

Eisenhower Matrix: This technique involves prioritizing your tasks and commitments – a crucial life skill.

1. Make a list of all your tasks and activities for the day or week.
2. On a piece of paper, draw a large square and divide it into four quadrants. (Show the Eisenhower Matrix)
3. In the first quadrant, add urgent and important tasks, like completing your studies on an immediate deadline or finishing up your backlog. You should aim to clear this quadrant right away.
4. The second quadrant will contain important non-urgent tasks, like your extracurricular activities. Schedule this list after finishing the first quadrant.
5. The urgent but unimportant tasks go in the third quadrant, like club meetings or sudden hangout plans. Check this list only after completing the first one and if it doesn't interfere with the second one.
6. You may have already guessed that the final quadrant will contain tasks that are neither urgent nor important, like time-wasting habits or distractions. Avoid these things to free up your time for more important tasks.

Pomodoro Technique: This is a powerful scheduling technique that maintains your focus throughout multiple activities and tasks. It involves studying or doing extracurriculars for a specific time, taking a short break, and resuming the activity. The longer you focus on an activity, the lesser your focus becomes. The short break helps you recharge so you can maintain your focus for longer periods.

The ideal activity period is 25 minutes, and the break time is five minutes. You can change these times according to your preferences (say, an hour of study followed by a 10-minute break). Furthermore, after every four sessions, you can take a longer break to recuperate better.

50/30/20 Rule: The 50/30/20 rule is a financial technique, but it can be applied to time management, too. Set 50% of your time for studies, 30% for extracurriculars, and 20% for other kinds of fun. For instance, you generally have 14 hours per day, excluding the time for essentials like meals, bathing, etc. Of these, you can spend seven hours studying, four hours on extracurriculars, and three hours on doing other things.

Setting Realistic Goals

If none of the aforementioned tips and techniques are working for you, try to reevaluate your goals. Are you taking more courses and doing more extracurriculars than you can handle? Set realistic goals for yourself with the help of the following tips:

- **Be SMART About Your Goals:** Here, SMART is an acronym for Specific, Measurable, Achievable, Relevant, and Time-bound. Clearly define your goals. Instead of saying, "You want to improve your grades," say, "You want to improve your grades by one level."

They should be measurable so you can track your progress and know when you've achieved them. Instead of saying, "You want to study more," specify a measurable goal like "You want to spend two hours studying for each subject every day."

Achievable implies that the goals are within your reach and align with your abilities, resources, and time constraints – not just achievable in general. If you have been getting a 'C' grade so far, don't be overambitious and set a goal for an 'A.' Take it one step at a time and aim for a 'B' first.

Ensure your goals are relevant to your overall objectives, aspirations, and interests. They should align with your academic interests, career goals, and personal values. If you're not interested in a particular extracurricular activity and are doing it due to peer pressure, quit doing it and take up something more relevant in its place.

Finally, time-bound means setting schedules and deadlines and sticking to them. Overcommitting will cause you to miss deadlines, and your schedule will become chaotic. Set deadlines that you can achieve. Don't try to impress your peers and professors by committing to an unrealistic schedule.

- **Break Down Larger Goals:** Is your goal so big that it seems unrealistic at the moment? Don't discard it just yet. It may not be unrealistic, but it may require a lot of time to achieve. See if you can break it down into smaller, more immediately achievable goals. Manage your time for those smaller goals while keeping the larger picture in mind.
- **Consider Your Priorities:** Realistic goals always take your priorities into account. At this age, your priority will be your health and academic performance in equal measure. Fun extracurriculars are important, but they will come after your first priority. State your extracurricular goals based on your studies and well-being.

The Art of Saying "No"

Saying a simple "No" will balance your studies and fun, along with many other aspects of your life.
https://www.pexels.com/photo/red-and-black-no-text-4069665/

Did you know that while balancing fun and studies, almost all the hurdles vanish if you learn to say "No" to things that don't help you reach your goals? One of your goals may be to spend time with your friends, but do you *really need to smoke while doing so*? It doesn't help with any of your goals but hinders them by causing potential health problems in the future. Saying a simple "No" will balance your studies and fun, along with many other aspects of your life.

- **Time Management:** You have limited time to balance your academic responsibilities, extracurricular activities, social life, and personal interests. Saying "No" to non-essential commitments allows you to prioritize your time effectively and focus on tasks that align with your goals.
- **Avoiding Overcommitment:** By declining excessive commitments, you can prevent burnout and improve your health. Overcommitting to too many activities or obligations can lead to stress, exhaustion, and decreased academic performance.
- **Setting Boundaries:** Healthy boundaries in any relationship include a fair share of "No"s. You can assert your needs and prioritize self-care without feeling guilty or obligated to please others at the expense of your well-being.
- **Maintaining Focus:** When you say "No" to distractions, unnecessary tasks, or requests that do not pertain to your goals, you can maintain better focus on your studies and academic pursuits. This also helps you spend more time having fun.
- **Respecting Priorities:** Saying "No" reinforces the importance of prioritizing academic and personal goals. It teaches you to value your time and energy and to make choices that support your long-term success and well-being.
- **Building Self-Confidence:** This empowers you to make decisions that serve your best interests as you learn to stand up for yourself in various situations.
- **Avoiding Negative Influences:** Saying "No" to peer pressure, unhealthy habits, or activities that may hinder academic progress or personal growth is essential. It helps you stay true to your values and make positive choices for your future.
- **Making Yourself Independent:** The simple act of saying "No" speaks volumes about your independence. It implies you think critically and make independent decisions. It cultivates a sense of autonomy and self-reliance, which are essential skills for success in both academic and professional settings.

However, this doesn't mean you should keep saying "No" to every opportunity that knocks on your door. Even if something doesn't align with your goals, it may give you a chance to set a new goal that complements your existing ones. Keep yourself open to opportunities, but don't hesitate to say "No" if it doesn't feel right.

Extracurricular activities pave the way for several opportunities that would enhance the personal, academic, and professional aspects of your life in and beyond college. You can acquire new skills, connect with new people, and find new goals to accomplish. You also add more talents to your resume, develop leadership potential, and prepare yourself for the real world.

These benefits of extracurriculars may or may not be useful later in life, but the memories you make during this time will stay with you forever. Put the tips and techniques mentioned in this chapter into practice, and you will make more new memories by effectively balancing fun and studies.

Chapter 6: Strategies for Test-Taking and Stress-Busting

Whether it's midterm or final exams, assessments like these can bring with them a surge of stress and anxiety. The pressure to understand, memorize, and recall extensive course material, along with the juggling act of multiple subjects, creates an overwhelming sense of academic strain. You're not alone in this, as many of your peers likely experience similar emotions. When dealing with exams, the first thing you must do is break down the material into more manageable portions. Dealing with one section at a time makes it easier to focus and the task less daunting.

The next step involves crafting a realistic study schedule that includes breaks and prioritizes tasks. This is crucial for effective time management and steers you away from stress-inducing last-minute cramming. Furthermore, prioritizing self-care, including sufficient sleep, a balanced diet, and activities promoting well-being, is also pivotal during these high-pressure periods. Remember, it's okay to seek support from friends, family, or classmates, as their perspectives and encouragement can be invaluable.

Craft a realistic study schedule that includes breaks and prioritizes tasks.
https://www.pexels.com/photo/crop-woman-taking-notes-in-calendar-5239917/

Embracing mindfulness techniques and relaxation exercises should also be incorporated into your daily routine. They help manage stress in the moment while maintaining a balanced view of your broader educational journey. In this chapter, you will learn everything in detail so you can study effectively and make the most of your time, all without stress.

Crafting a Strategic Study Plan

As you start preparing for exams, it's essential to begin with a well-thought-out study plan. Instead of jumping from one subject to another, break down the material you need to cover into manageable sections, allocating your study sessions to specific topics. Targeting certain topics facilitates a more thorough understanding and makes tracking your progress easier. Allocate realistic timeframes to each section, ensuring a balanced distribution of effort across all subjects.

Utilizing Effective Note-Taking Methods

Your notes are a powerful tool for comprehension and revision. Instead of making lecture notes word by word during the class, focus on capturing key concepts, examples, and explanations. Consider employing techniques such as the Cornell method, which divides your note page into sections for main ideas, details, and a summary. Condense information, use bullet points, and highlight crucial points to make your notes a concise and effective study resource.

Active Learning Strategies

Rather than passively reading, use flashcards, concept mapping, or teaching the material to someone else. These strategies are the same as you previously learned in chapter 2 of this book. Another strategy is to quiz yourself periodically to reinforce what you've learned. Active learning not only solidifies your grasp of the subject matter but also makes the study process more dynamic and engaging.

Establishing a Revision Routine

Without a regular revision routine, retaining topics long-term might become difficult. Schedule periodic review sessions throughout your study plan to revisit previously covered material. Recalling already covered topics solidifies your knowledge and builds a strong foundation as you progress through the curriculum.

Incorporating Multisensory Techniques

Try using multiple senses in your study process to enhance memory. For example, you can utilize visual aids like charts, diagrams, and graphs to understand theoretical information better. Likewise, you can listen to relevant podcasts or recordings about your study topic to reinforce auditory learning. By appealing to different senses, you create a more comprehensive and memorable learning experience.

Mindful Breaks and Rewards

No matter what learning strategy you practice, taking short, mindful breaks in your study routine will always be necessary to maintain focus and prevent burnout.

Flexibility and Adaptability

Recognize that no single study strategy fits all. Be flexible in adapting your methods based on the material you are studying, your learning style, and feedback from your progress. Furthermore, experimenting with different techniques can pinpoint the ones that work best for you, promoting a more personalized and effective study approach.

While you will find many other strategies and techniques like these, the key to success is implementing these techniques correctly.

The Power of Starting Early

Starting your midterm preparation early on can be a game-changer. By distributing your study efforts over an extended period, you can reduce last-minute stress as you will develop a deeper understanding of the material. Starting early will also give you time for regular revision, making the information more likely to stick in the long run.

Midterm Study Planner Template

To organize your study and start early preparation, consider making a midterm study planner. You can make a customizable tool to structure your study schedule and make it more manageable. Here is a template you can follow for inspiration. Furthermore, please remember that you can add or omit any of the subheadings to better match your schedule.

Daily Goals:

- To keep your focus, set achievable daily study goals and track progress.
- Prioritize specific topics or chapters for each day based on their importance.

Topics to Cover:

- Always divide the material into manageable sections or themes.
- Assign specific topics to each study session to maintain clarity and avoid getting overwhelmed.

Self-Care Reminders:

- Always add self-care elements to your daily planner to keep your health in check.
- Schedule breaks, meals, and moments for relaxation to prevent burnout.
- Allocate specific time blocks for each study session, ensuring a balanced distribution of subjects.
- Use the planner to track your progress. Celebrate achievements, and adjust your schedule if needed.

Benefits of the Midterm Study Planner

- Provides a clear roadmap for your study journey, minimizing ambiguity and stress.
- Facilitates an early start to the preparation process, ensuring ample time for understanding and retention.
- Balanced Approach: Enables a balanced distribution of study efforts across all subjects, avoiding the pitfalls of last-minute cramming.
- Integrates self-care reminders to promote a holistic approach to exam preparation, emphasizing the importance of maintaining your mental and physical health.

Creating a personalized midterm study planner will keep your study schedule organized while keeping your health in optimum condition. Remember, starting early and breaking down the material into manageable sections are keys to success, contributing to a more confident and less stressful exam experience.

Approaching Different Types of Exam Questions

Multiple-Choice Questions (MCQs)

Begin by thoroughly reading the question stem. Without immediately looking at the choices, attempt to answer independently. This keeps the distractions at bay. Once you have a tentative answer, examine each choice, eliminating those that are clearly incorrect. If uncertain, mark the question for review and move on, returning after you have attempted other questions.

Tip: Pay attention to the language of the question. Absolute terms like always or never often indicate incorrect options. Furthermore, if two choices seem correct, consider the one that is more comprehensive or relevant.

True/False Questions

Read the statements thoroughly. True/false questions are often misleading, so read each word carefully. If any part of the statement is false, mark it as such. If unsure, remember that generally, statements are more likely to be true than false.

Tip: Be cautious with double negatives, as they can introduce confusion. Simplify the statement to its basic components to clarify the intended meaning.

Short Answer and Fill-in-the-Blank Questions

Take your time and carefully read the question, ensuring you grasp the specific information required. Provide your answer concisely and clearly. Review your answer for accuracy, paying attention to spelling and grammar.

Tip: If uncertain about a detail, offer as much relevant information as possible. Partial credit is often awarded for demonstrating partial knowledge.

Essay Questions

Strategy: To structure your thoughts, begin by outlining your response. Ensure your essay includes an introduction, body, and conclusion. Then, address each component of the question methodically, providing evidence to support your arguments.

Tip: Be clear and coherent in your writing. Use examples and add topic details to strengthen your arguments. Don't forget to proofread your response for grammatical accuracy before moving on.

Mindfulness Exercises for Exam Anxiety

Deep Breathing

It's a technique to calm down your nerves, allowing the mind to tap into a stress-free zone. Find a place to sit comfortably, preferably on a ground mat. Close your eyes, and take a slow, deep breath through your nose, expanding your diaphragm. Hold your breath for a few seconds, then exhale slowly through your mouth. Repeat this process, keeping the focus on your breath. This exercise regulates your nervous system and promotes a sense of calm.

Body Scan Meditation

Lie down or sit in a comfortable position. Direct your attention to each part of your body, starting from your toes and moving up to your head. It can pinpoint any tension or discomfort in the body.

Guided Imagery

Close your eyes and visualize a peaceful place, whether it's a beach, a forest, or mountains. Activate your senses by imagining the sights, sounds, and smells of this serene location. This mental escape helps alleviate anxiety and provides a moment of tranquility.

Mindful Breathing with Counting

Inhale slowly, counting to four, and then exhale for a count of six. Focus your attention on the breath and the counting process. This elongated exhale triggers the body's relaxation response, easing stress and tension.

Physical Activities to Relieve Exam Anxiety

Quick Walk or Stretching Break

Take a short break during study sessions to go for a brisk walk or do some light stretching. These activities will increase blood flow, release tension, and keep you healthy.

Yoga or Tai Chi

You can also opt for yoga or tai chi sessions. These practices combine gentle movements with deep breathing, promoting relaxation and mindfulness. If you don't have the time, many online resources are available that offer short and beginner-friendly routines.

Progressive Muscle Relaxation (PMR)

Sit or lie down comfortably. Starting from your toes, tense each muscle group for a few seconds and then release. Gradually work your way up to your head. Activating each muscle group can release physical tension and identify areas of strain. The technique is similar to the body scan, but the main difference is that in PMR, you consciously *try to relax the areas under strain.*

Fidgeting with Stress Balls

Sometimes, stress can build up to the roof, making it difficult to maintain focus. In times like these, playing with a stress ball or a fidgeting toy can come in handy. You can use it during study breaks or moments of anxiety to channel nervous energy and release tension through gentle squeezing.

Mindful Eating

During breaks, be mindful of what you eat. Focus on the taste, texture, and sensation of each bite. This provides a mental break and encourages a mindful, present mindset.

Nature Breaks

Activity: Spend a few minutes outdoors, whether it's in a nearby park or simply sitting on a balcony. Connecting with nature can have a calming effect and provide a mental reset.

Journaling

Write down your thoughts and feelings in a journal. This practice can help you process emotions, identify sources of stress, and gain perspective on exam-related concerns.

Remember, incorporating these relaxation techniques and activities into your routine can contribute to a more balanced and resilient approach to exam preparation. Find what works best for you and make self-care a priority during the challenging exam period.

Incorporating Relaxation Practices into Daily Routines during Midterms

The intensity of the midterm period demands not only academic focus but also mindful self-care. Embracing relaxation practices as integral components of your daily routine can significantly contribute to managing stress and maintaining a balanced mindset. Here's how you can seamlessly integrate these practices into your hectic schedule:

Morning Mindfulness

Morning mindfulness.
https://www.pexels.com/photo/calm-woman-in-lotus-pose-meditating-after-awakening-at-home-3791634/

Start your day with a brief mindfulness exercise. Before diving into study materials, take a few moments to practice deep breathing or a quick body scan meditation. This will set a positive tone for the day and establish a centered mindset.

Mindful Study Breaks

Schedule regular study breaks and use these intervals for brief mindfulness exercises or physical activities. Whether it's a few minutes of guided imagery or a short walk, these breaks rejuvenate your mind, preventing burnout and improving overall concentration.

Lunchtime Relaxation

Incorporate mindfulness into your lunch routine. Practice mindful eating by savoring each bite and taking a moment to appreciate your food. Use this time to disconnect from screens and focus on nourishing your body and mind.

Afternoon Stretch or Yoga Session

Amid the demands of midday studies, allocate a short period for stretching or a brief yoga session. Online platforms can offer quick routines for people with busy schedules, helping release tension and promoting mental clarity.

Evening Relaxation Ritual

Wind down your day with a calming ritual. Engage in a longer mindfulness exercise, such as guided meditation or progressive muscle relaxation, to release any accumulated tension. Consider a warm bath or gentle stretching before bedtime to promote relaxation.

Bedtime Reflection

Reflect on your day before bedtime. Consider jotting down a few positive moments, challenges you've overcome, or things you're grateful for in a journal. This practice shifts your focus toward positivity and fosters a sense of accomplishment.

Mindful Transition to Sleep

Adopt a mindful approach as you transition to sleep. Practice deep breathing or listen to calming music to ease into a restful state. Limit exposure to screens before bedtime to ensure a more peaceful and rejuvenating sleep.

Weekly Check-In

Set aside a specific time each week for a more extended self-care check-in. Reflect on your well-being, adjust your routines if necessary, and celebrate your achievements, both academically and in incorporating these relaxation practices.

Consistency is key when incorporating relaxation practices into your daily routine. Choose practices that resonate with you and adapt them to fit your schedule. These mindful moments not only help manage exam anxiety but also contribute to your overall well-being during the hectic midterm period. By prioritizing self-care, you enhance your resilience and optimize your capacity to navigate academic challenges with a clearer and more focused mind.

Digital Study Tools

Flashcard Apps: Utilize digital apps that support flashcards for effective memorization. You can also find various flashcard quizzes to optimize your study time and repetition.

Online Study Communities

Join online forums or communities dedicated to academic discussions. These spaces allow for collaborative learning and information exchange. You can also initiate a discussion on study-related topics and even get already-discussed answers for common queries you may have.

E-Learning Platforms

Explore digital platforms that offer supplementary courses to deepen your understanding of specific topics. These resources can provide alternative explanations and additional study materials.

Educational Videos: Leverage educational video content available on various platforms to gain visual insights into complex subjects.

Productivity Tools

Task Management Apps: Use digital tools to organize your study tasks and break down your study plan into manageable steps to enhance productivity.

Focus Apps: Employ applications that discourage multitasking and promote focused study sessions.

Virtual Libraries and Resources

Digital Libraries: Access e-books and digital resources through online libraries and platforms. These resources provide quick and convenient access to relevant materials.

Online Journals and Articles: Stay updated with the latest research using academic databases available on the internet.

Mobile Learning Applications

Language Learning Tools: Consider language learning apps or online resources as a refreshing study break. Learning a new language can activate different cognitive skills.

Audio Content: Listen to educational podcasts or audiobooks during commutes or short breaks to enhance your understanding of various subjects.

Wellness Tools

Mindfulness Apps: Explore digital tools that offer guided meditation sessions to alleviate stress and enhance focus.

Fitness Apps: Utilize fitness applications for guided workouts or physical activity, which is essential for stress relief.

Gamified Learning Platforms

Educational Games: Engage with gamified learning platforms that turn studying into an interactive experience. These platforms often incorporate quizzes and challenges for self-assessment.

Time Management Solutions

Pomodoro Technique Apps: Explore applications that implement the Pomodoro Technique, breaking study sessions into focused intervals followed by short breaks. This method enhances productivity while preventing burnout.

Calendar Tools: To manage your time effectively, integrate your study sessions into digital calendars and set reminders for upcoming exams.

Leveraging technology strategically can transform your study routine, making it more efficient, collaborative, and engaging. Select tools that align with your learning preferences and needs, ensuring that technology becomes a supportive component of your successful midterm preparation.

Navigating the challenges of midterms involves a holistic approach that combines effective study strategies, mindful self-care, and the strategic use of technology. By recognizing the common feelings of anxiety and stress, you can incorporate relaxation techniques into their daily routines. From mindfulness exercises to digital study tools, the amalgamation of these practices not only alleviates stress but also enhances exam preparation. The detailed study strategies, coupled with the integration of technology, act as valuable resources for students seeking a balanced and resilient approach to the demands of midterm exams.

Chapter 7: Making Friends and Influencing People

Remember the days in high school when you practically knew everyone? You had your clique, your squad, and you knew the drill. But now, as you get ready to step into college life, onto a campus where you'll encounter a whole new universe of faces, it's suddenly like you're back in kindergarten – nervous but also excited to meet new people and make friends. Maybe you'll recognize a few people from back in the day, or maybe you're diving into this sea of strangers entirely solo. It's a thrilling thought, isn't it? Maybe you'll meet a globetrotter from halfway across the world, bump into a laid-back surfer dude, or maybe even strike up a conversation with a DJ, a passionate writer, a singer, or just someone taking it easy – because let's face it, it takes all sorts to fill up a college campus.

Extend that hand of friendship to your fellow freshmen.
https://www.pexels.com/photo/photograph-of-a-group-of-students-talking-with-each-other-7972537/

Now, diving into this social whirlwind might seem daunting. It's perfectly normal to feel those butterflies fluttering in your stomach. However, there's no secret handshake or grand entrance needed to introduce yourself. Just remember, there are heaps of other people in the same boat, feeling just as uncertain as you are. So, relax, be yourself, toss out a few friendly questions, and above all, just be kind. There's no script you have to follow here. One of the coolest things about college is that it's a blank canvas – you're free to paint yourself however you please. Maybe you were a wallflower or a bookworm in high school, but here's your chance to let your true colors shine.

Always follow the golden rule – acceptance. You do you, and let others do them. This isn't high school where everyone's history is common knowledge. Extend that hand of friendship to your fellow freshmen; after all, you're all in the same boat trying to figure out this whole "college" thing together.

Fitting In: Finding Your Place in College

Finding your groove in college can be like fitting into a new pair of shoes. Some people slide right in, while others need a little more time to break them in. But what about cliques? You might have thought you left those behind in high school, but surprise – they can still pop up in college.

Yep, even in college, there are cliques. Whether it's the cool kids hogging the TV lounge, the frat brothers dominating the dining hall, or the clique of Mean Girls giving you the side-eye as you pass by, they're still around. It's tempting to latch onto a group right away for that sense of security, but hold on a second.

It's okay to take your time and get to know different people. Don't rush into joining a clique before you've had a chance to see who's who. Some friendships might not be all they're cracked up to be, and you could end up missing out on better connections down the road.

Watch out for those who seem a bit too eager to pull you into their group. They might have their own agenda or be a little too needy for your liking. Trust your gut, and don't be afraid to keep your distance.

Fitting in doesn't mean squeezing into one clique and calling it a day. College is like a buffet – you've got options! You might find your study buddies in your dorm, your workout pals at the gym, your fellow bookworms in your classes, and your party crew at social events. Don't limit yourself to one small group – branch out and see what else is out there.

And hey, if your first year feels a bit like high school redux, don't sweat it. College is a big place, and there's room for everyone to find their people. Just keep an open mind, stay true to yourself, and don't be afraid to try new things.

Communication in College Life

The key to making friends lies in effective communication – a skill that not only helps you form meaningful connections but also fosters lasting friendships.

1. **Initiate Conversations**

    The first step in making friends is initiating conversations. Don't hesitate to strike up a chat with your classmates, dorm mates, or people at social events. Simple greetings like "Hey, how's it going?" or "What's your major?" can pave the way for meaningful interactions. You could start a conversation by complimenting someone's shirt or asking about their opinion on a recent class assignment. This shows that you're interested in getting to know them better.

2. **Active Listening**

   Listening attentively is crucial in building rapport with others. Show genuine interest in what your conversation partner is saying by maintaining eye contact, nodding, and asking follow-up questions. Avoid interrupting and give them space to express themselves. If a classmate shares their excitement about joining a club, you could respond with enthusiasm and ask about their role or upcoming events.

3. **Share Your Experiences**

   Opening up about your own experiences and interests allows others to relate to you on a personal level. Share anecdotes, hobbies, and aspirations to establish common ground and deepen connections. If you're passionate about photography, you could share a memorable moment you captured or discuss your favorite photography spots on campus.

4. **Attend Social Events**

   College campuses offer a myriad of social events, from club meetings to sports games and parties. Attend these gatherings to meet new people and expand your social circle. Step out of your comfort zone and embrace new experiences. If there's a campus-wide barbecue event, grab a plate of food and mingle with fellow students. Engage in casual conversations, participate in games, and exchange contact information to stay connected.

5. **Utilize Technology**

   In today's digital age, technology serves as a valuable tool for communication. Exchange contact information with new acquaintances and connect on social media platforms like Facebook, Instagram, or Snapchat to stay in touch outside of class. After a group study session, you could create a WhatsApp group to share notes, ask questions, or plan future study sessions.

6. **Be Genuine and Respectful**

   Authenticity is key to forming genuine friendships. Be yourself and treat others with respect and kindness. Avoid gossiping or engaging in negative behavior that could tarnish your reputation. If you encounter a disagreement or misunderstanding with a friend, address it calmly and respectfully. Effective communication involves listening to each other's perspectives and finding common ground to resolve conflicts.

7. **Follow-up**

   Building friendships requires effort and consistency. Follow up with new acquaintances by inviting them to grab coffee, study together, or attend campus events. Small gestures can go a long way in nurturing budding friendships. If you meet someone interesting in class, follow up with a friendly message expressing your enjoyment of their company and suggesting a study session or lunch together.

Conversation Cues

Stuck on how to break the ice with someone you've just met? Here are some cues tailor-made for college life:

- Waiting for the elevator together? Strike up a conversation about the dorm's latest menu or commiserate over the eternal wait for the said elevator. It's a strong bonding experience.

- Spot someone rocking their favorite team's gear? Dive into a discussion about their loyalty. Ask how long they've been a fan, what their favorite moments are, or even what their predictions are for the upcoming season.

- Notice a fellow student sporting a t-shirt from a high school musical, a service project, or a charity run? Show interest in their experiences. Ask about their involvement, where they participated, and what impact it had on them.
- Catch someone engrossed in a book? Use it as a conversation starter. Express curiosity about the book they're reading, share your thoughts on it if you've read it, or ask for recommendations for your next read.
- Running late and forgetting your syllabus? Don't panic. Strike up a conversation with a classmate on the way in. Politely ask if you can take a quick peek at theirs – chances are they'll understand the struggle and may even offer some insights into the class.
- If you notice someone wearing a shirt or carrying a flyer promoting a campus event, use it as an opportunity to strike up a conversation. Ask if they're planning to attend, what they're looking forward to, or if they've been to similar events in the past.
- Food is a universal language, especially in college. If you spot someone with a particularly appetizing snack or meal, compliment their choice and ask where they got it. Food-related conversations are always a hit.
- College students bond over shared academic experiences. If you're in the library or in a study group, comment on the workload or a challenging assignment. You can commiserate with tough professors or swap study tips.
- Every college has its unique quirks and traditions. If you encounter something unusual or interesting on campus, like a statue with a funny backstory or a quirky tradition, bring it up in conversation. Ask if they've heard about it or if they have any stories to share.
- College campuses are melting pots of diverse cultures and backgrounds. If you notice someone wearing clothing or accessories that reflect their cultural heritage, express interest in learning more about their background. Ask about their traditions, customs, or experiences growing up.
- If you notice someone listening to music, ask about their favorite bands or artists. You can also discuss recent movies, TV shows, or books that you've enjoyed and see if they share your tastes.
- If you see someone heading to the gym, attending a fitness class, or carrying a water bottle, ask about their workout routine or wellness practices. You can bond over shared fitness goals or exchange tips for staying healthy on campus.

Get to Know People on Your Floor

Your first encounter with new faces? You can bet it'll be in your dorm. Sure, you'll eventually run into people in class, the library, or maybe even the local watering hole, but your dorm is like ground zero for making connections. It's where the friendships of tomorrow begin. So, keep these tips in mind to make friends in your dorm.

- Keep your dorm room door propped open, at least in the first few days when you move in.
- Rally the troops for a mealtime adventure. Whether it's hitting up the campus cafeteria or venturing off campus to try out a new eatery, turning it into a weekly tradition can bond your floor like nothing else. Theme nights, anyone?

- Got a knack for gaming? Organize some friendly competition on your Xbox or PlayStation. Better yet, why not host a full-blown gaming tournament? The more, the merrier – it's a surefire way to get everyone in on the action and spark some camaraderie.
- Dive into the world of fantasy sports! Start a free online league for football in the fall or baseball in the spring. It's not just about the game; it's about the banter and bonding over shared victories and defeats.
- Shake things up by organizing group outings to see a comedian, catch a live band, or attend a campus theater production. Embrace the unique experiences your campus has to offer and make memories together.
- A simple smile can go a long way. Strike up conversations on the floor or in the community bathroom, or chat with someone in the elevator – just be open to connecting with anyone and everyone.
- Keep that door adorned with your name tag and a message board. You can also add pictures of you and your roommate. It's a personal touch that adds warmth and personality to your living space.
- In a world dominated by screens, make an effort to have real, face-to-face interactions. Don't rely solely on technology to communicate with your roommate or floormates. Nothing beats good old-fashioned conversation.

Challenge yourself to step out of your comfort zone. Make an effort to connect with people outside your immediate circle. Don't let the layout of your floor or building dictate your friendships – reach out and bridge the gap.

Fraternities and Sororities

Frats and sororities have been around since way back in the 1700s. Back then, students started them up to get their friends involved in activities outside of classes. Fast forward to today, and some folks swear by Greek life, saying it's all about making lifelong friends and stepping up as leaders. In some cases, that can be the case. But let's be real – some Greek groups these days are just excuses to party hard and pull off risky stunts. Do you know how every crew has its own slang? Well, fraternities and sororities are no different. Here's the 4-1-1 on the basics you'll likely hear:

- **Active:** A fully-fledged member.
- **Bid:** An invite to join.
- **Brothers/Sisters:** What they call each other.
- **Chapter:** A local branch.
- **Fraternity/Sorority:** Clubs for college peeps.
- **Hazing:** Tests and pranks (which, FYI, many campuses have cracked down on).
- **Legacy:** If your fam's been in, you're in.
- **Open-house Parties:** Quick hangouts to check out the scene.
- **Rush:** The big recruitment week.
- **Pan-Hellenic Council:** The bosses overseeing all the Greek groups.

So, forget what you've seen in movies like Animal House. These days, Greek life is more about safety and fitting in with modern norms. The fun starts with rush week, a whirlwind of events to find new members. Joining a frat or sorority usually means going through a formal, informal, or summer rush. Formals are before or at the start of the semester, and informals are right after (and sometimes in the summer after the spring semester). *Each group picks its vibe.*

Rush week kicks off with open-house parties, where you scope out different places. Then, fancy invites to longer, fancier parties arrive. Finally, if you're seen as a top pick, you'll be asked to the last round, where they really try to seal the deal.

Being part of a Greek group can mean making lifelong friends, learning leadership chops, and getting a built-in social network. But, let's be real – rush week can be stressful, and getting rejected? Ouch. Plus, it can hit your wallet hard, and balancing parties with classes isn't always easy. In the end, deciding to pledge or not is a personal call. Weighing up the pros and cons, thinking about the pressures you're feeling, and asking yourself if it lines up with your vibe and goals are the keys.

Embracing Diversity

Expanding your horizons is rewarding and helps you grow as a person.
https://www.pexels.com/photo/group-of-students-talking-at-a-staircase-8199169/

Living in a college community opens doors to new ideas, perspectives, and ways of living. It's a melting pot of cultures, religions, abilities, sexual orientations, races, and genders. So, how do you navigate this sea of differences?

- Challenge yourself to interact with people from different backgrounds.
- Listen to different viewpoints and be open to new ways of thinking.
- Allow yourself to be challenged and inspired by your peers' unique experiences.
- Take an interest in different cultures and ways of life.
- Admit that there's a lot you don't know, and be willing to learn.

It can feel overwhelming to be surrounded by so much diversity, but the key is to have an open mind. Recognize your biases and be willing to ask questions. Here are some simple ways to start:

- Ask about holidays and traditions celebrated by others.
- Inquire about the meaning of unique names.
- Learn about different backgrounds and experiences.
- Strike up conversations in common areas.
- Attend cultural events and festivals.
- Learn a few phrases in a different language.

Expanding your horizons is rewarding and helps you grow as a person. As this world becomes more diverse, embracing differences will be crucial for success in life. Inclusivity is essential for creating a welcoming community where everyone feels accepted. Here are some tips to foster inclusivity:

- Use inclusive language and avoid assumptions.
- Respect different family structures and relationships.
- Acknowledge and celebrate diverse holidays and religions.
- Avoid harmful language and stereotypes.
- Break free from gender norms and biases.
- Be mindful of cultural sensitivities and avoid making fun of others.

Being inclusive isn't always easy, but it's worth the effort. Remember, everyone deserves to feel welcomed and valued.

Identifying Toxic Friendships

Just as campuses are filled with wonderful individuals, some might not have your best interests at heart. Here are six types of toxic friendships to be wary of:

1. **The Constant Crisis**

   If you find yourself always lending an ear to your friends' problems without receiving the same support in return, or if your friend seems to be in perpetual turmoil, it might be time to seek new connections. Friendship should involve mutual support – not one-sided crises. For example, you spend hours consoling your friend about their relationship issues, but when you need someone to talk to, they're nowhere to be found.

2. **The Joker**

   Friendly teasing is fine, but if you're constantly the target of hurtful jokes or if your friends can dish it out but can't take it, it's time to distance yourself and seek companions who treat you with kindness. Example: Your friends laugh at your expense, making you feel embarrassed or belittled instead of uplifted.

3. **The Furious Friend**

   Any friendship that involves violence, whether physical or verbal, is unhealthy. Don't tolerate friends who resort to throwing things or using aggression to resolve conflicts. Example: Your friend loses their temper easily and throws objects when upset, creating a hostile environment.

4. **The Liability**

   If you always find yourself cleaning up after your friends' messes or constantly worrying about their well-being, it's a sign that the friendship is unbalanced. While occasional slip-ups are normal, habitual irresponsibility is a red flag. Example: You're left cleaning up after your friend's wild party while they stumble off to bed, oblivious to the chaos they've caused.

5. **The "No" Friend**

   Friendships should involve compromise and mutual interests. If you feel like you're always doing what your friends want without them considering your preferences, it's time to seek out companions who value your input. For example, your friends always dictate where to go and what to do, leaving you feeling sidelined and unappreciated.

6. **The Arm-Twister**

   Beware of friends who pressure you into activities that go against your values or make you feel guilty for not complying. Healthy friends should respect your boundaries and support your decisions. Example: Your friends mock you for not wanting to participate in risky behavior, making you feel out of place for standing firm in your beliefs.

Disengaging from Toxic Friendships

If you find yourself entangled in a toxic friendship, here are three ways to disengage:

- Stay busy by participating in new activities to meet different people and distance yourself from toxic friends. Focus on your interests and commitments, making it clear that your time is valuable. For instance, you can try joining a club or a sports team to expand your social circle.

- Invite toxic friends to group outings to alleviate the pressure of one-on-one interactions. Encourage them to mingle with new people. For example, you could organize a group movie night or game day, inviting both your toxic friends and other acquaintances to join.

- Communicate honestly. Express your feelings directly to the friend you wish to distance yourself from, emphasizing your need for personal growth and positive influences. Calmly explain to your friend that you're seeking new experiences and connections that align with your goals and values.

Navigating friendships in college boils down to one thing: communication. Whether you're striking up conversations in class, attending social events, or connecting through technology, effective communication is the glue that bonds friendships together. So, don't be afraid to step out of your comfort zone, make new friends, and create lasting memories. College is a journey best shared with others, and with the right communication skills, your social circle will thrive, making your college years truly unforgettable.

Chapter 8: Budgeting Bliss: Managing Money without Missing Out

As a student, managing finances can feel like navigating a maze with limited resources and numerous temptations along the way. Two of the most common challenges you're likely to encounter are dealing with tight budgets and resisting impulsive spending. Although a stipend from scholarships, earning from part-time jobs, or getting financial support can cover essential expenses like tuition, rent, and groceries, it all requires using the right money management strategies.

Whether it's dining out, buying gadgets, or splurging on social activities, these activities can quickly drain your funds and lead to financial stress. To avoid getting into such a situation, it's crucial to recognize the importance of financial responsibility and develop good money management skills early on. Understanding your income sources, tracking expenses, creating a realistic budget, and finding ways to save can make it easier to navigate financial constraints more effectively.

It's crucial to recognize the importance of financial responsibility and develop good money management skills early on.
https://www.pexels.com/photo/man-in-black-beanie-hat-holding-money-6328888/

Furthermore, you have to master self-control by understanding the psychology of impulse spending, the necessity of setting clear financial goals, creating a spending plan, and keeping track of expenditures. All these steps help you resist the temptation to overspend.

Being financially responsible isn't just about surviving as a student; it's about laying the groundwork for a brighter future. Please remember that it takes time to learn about personal finance, develop good money habits, and set short-term and long-term goals. Be patient and maintain a learning attitude to build a foundation for long-term success.

Taking Control of Your Finances

Tracking Expenses

The first thing you need to do is to start documenting all your expenses over a defined period, whether it's a week or a month. This includes everything from rent and groceries to entertainment and transportation. You can use a notebook, spreadsheet, or budgeting app to track your expenses. The goal is to gain a clear understanding of where your money is going and identify areas where you can cut back.

Identifying Necessary vs. Discretionary Spending

Once you've tracked your expenses, categorize them into necessary and discretionary spending. Necessary expenses are essential for your basic needs, like housing, food, transportation, and utilities. Discretionary spending, on the other hand, includes non-essential items like dining out, entertainment, and shopping. This distinction helps you prioritize your spending and identify areas where you need to control the expenses.

Creating a Realistic Budget

Based on your tracked expenses and income, create a realistic budget that allocates funds for necessary expenses first. Start by covering fixed costs like rent and utilities, followed by variable expenses like groceries and transportation. If your budget allows and you have a student loan to pay, you can also allocate funds for savings and debt repayment. The key is to balance your income with your expenses while leaving room for discretionary spending.

Finding Ways to Save Money on Everyday Expenses

Now that you have a budget in place, it's time to find ways to save money on everyday expenses. Consider the following tips:

Meal Planning and Cooking: Planning your meals ahead of time and cooking in your hostel can save you a significant amount of money compared to eating out. Many hostels have a dedicated kitchen space where with the necessary utensils to prepare your meals. However, don't forget to do your groceries before stepping in. Look for budget-friendly, quick, and healthy recipes to save time.

Using Student Discounts: Take advantage of student discounts whenever possible. Many retailers, restaurants, and entertainment venues offer discounts to students, so always ask if they have special pricing for students.

Limiting Impulse Purchases: Before making a purchase, especially a non-essential one, consider whether it aligns with your budget and financial goals. Stick to your budget and prioritize needs over wants to avoid impulsive spending.

Shopping Smart: Whether you're buying textbooks, electronics, or clothing, always compare prices and look for deals. Consider buying used or refurbished items to save money without sacrificing quality.

Minimizing Transportation Costs: If possible, walk, bike, or use public transportation instead of hailing a cab or driving. This can help you save money on gas, parking, and maintenance costs associated with owning a car.

Setting Up Automated Savings

Consider setting up automated transfers from your checking account to your savings account each month. This pay-yourself-first approach ensures that you're prioritizing savings by setting aside a portion of your income before you have a chance to spend it. Start with a small amount and gradually increase it over time as your financial situation improves.

Utilizing Cash Envelopes

An effective way to control unnecessary spending is by using the cash envelope system. Allocate a specific amount of cash to each budget category, such as groceries, dining out, and entertainment, and place the cash in separate envelopes. Once the cash in each envelope is gone for the month, you can't spend any more in that category until the next month. This helps you stay disciplined and avoid overspending.

Monitoring and Adjusting Your Budget

Budgeting is not a one-time task; it's an ongoing process that requires regular monitoring and adjustments. Periodically review your budget to see how well you're sticking to it and make adjustments as needed. If you find that you're consistently overspending in certain categories, consider reallocating funds from less essential areas or finding additional ways to cut costs.

Avoiding High-Interest Debt

Cost of Borrowing

High-interest debt, such as credit card debt or payday loans, has exorbitant interest rates that can quickly accumulate. The longer you carry the debt, the more interest you pay, which can significantly increase the total cost of borrowing. This means that even a small amount of debt can balloon into a substantial financial burden over time.

Financial Stress

Carrying high-interest debt can lead to significant financial stress and anxiety. Constantly worrying about making minimum payments, managing multiple creditors, and struggling to keep up with interest charges can take a toll on your mental and emotional well-being. Financial stress can also impact other areas of your life, including relationships, work performance, and overall quality of life.

Hinders to Financial Goals

High-interest debt can hinder your ability to achieve important financial goals, such as buying a home, starting a business, or saving for retirement. A large portion of your income may go toward servicing debt, leaving little room for saving and investing in your future. Furthermore, high levels of debt can negatively impact your credit score, making it more difficult to qualify for favorable loan terms in the future.

Trap of Debt Cycle

High-interest debt can trap you in a vicious cycle of borrowing and repayment. If you're unable to pay off the debt in full each month, you may find yourself carrying a balance and accruing more interest over time. This can make it increasingly challenging to break free from debt and can prolong your financial struggles indefinitely.

Opportunity Cost

Every dollar spent on high-interest debt is a dollar that could have been used for more productive purposes, such as building an emergency fund, investing in education or skills development, or saving for long-term goals. By avoiding high-interest debt, you free up resources that can be allocated toward wealth-building activities and improving your financial future.

Avoiding high-interest debt is essential for maintaining financial health, reducing stress, and achieving long-term financial success. By living within your means, budgeting effectively, and prioritizing debt repayment, you can break free from the cycle of debt and work toward a more secure and prosperous future.

Remember, it's not about depriving yourself of enjoyment; it's about making informed decisions and prioritizing your spending to align with your values and long-term objectives.

Setting Up the Budget Planner

Choose Your Format

Decide whether you want to use a physical planner, a spreadsheet, or a budgeting app. Each option has its pros and cons, so choose the format that works best for you.

Determine Your Categories

Identify the key categories that will encompass your expenses. Common categories include:
- Housing (rent, mortgage, utilities)
- Food (groceries, dining out)
- Transportation (gas, public transit, car maintenance)
- Health (insurance premiums, medications)
- Education (tuition, textbooks)
- Entertainment (movies, concerts, hobbies)
- Savings (emergency fund, retirement savings, other goals)

Allocate Space for Each Category

Create dedicated sections or columns in your planner for each expense category. Leave enough space to write down the details of your expenses within each category.

Determine Your Income Sources

List all sources of income for the month, including wages from part-time jobs, allowances, scholarships, grants, and any other form of financial support.

Using the Budget Planner

Record Your Income
At the beginning of the month, write down the total amount of income you expect to receive. Be realistic and include all sources of income, even irregular ones.

Estimate Your Expenses
Estimate how much you plan to spend in each expense category for the month. Start with fixed expenses like rent and utilities, then move on to variable expenses like groceries and entertainment.

Document Your Expenses
As the month progresses, record all your expenses in the corresponding categories. Be diligent about tracking every purchase, no matter how small. Use receipts, bank statements, or mobile banking apps to ensure accuracy.

Review and Adjust
Periodically review your budget planner to see how your actual expenses compare to your estimates. Are you staying within your budget, or are you overspending in certain areas? Adjust your spending habits and budget as needed to stay on track.

Analyze Your Spending Patterns
At the end of the month, take a closer look at your spending patterns. Did you stick to your budget, or did you overspend in certain categories? Identify any areas where you can cut back and make adjustments for the following month.

Set Goals and Track Progress
Use the budget planner to set specific financial goals, such as saving for a vacation or paying off debt. Break down your goals into smaller milestones and track your progress over time. Celebrate your achievements and adjust your budget as you work toward your goals.

Make Budgeting a Habit
Incorporate budgeting into your routine and make it a regular habit. Set aside time each week or month to update your budget planner, review your expenses, and plan for the future. The more consistent you are with budgeting, the better you'll become at managing your finances effectively.

By following these steps and using the budget planner consistently, you'll gain greater control over your finances, reduce financial stress, and work toward achieving your financial goals as a student. Remember, budgeting is a skill that takes time and practice to master, so be patient with yourself and stay committed to your financial success.

Making Extra Money in College

You can make extra money by babysitting.
https://www.pexels.com/photo/young-father-playing-with-his-baby-son-outdoors-4934420/

Part-Time Jobs

Explore both on-campus and off-campus job opportunities. On-campus jobs often offer flexibility and may include positions at the library, student center, or academic departments. Off-campus jobs could involve retail, hospitality, or customer service roles. Consider the proximity to your campus and the flexibility of the work schedule when choosing a job.

Internships

Look for internships related to your field of study, as they can provide valuable work experience and networking opportunities. Paid internships are ideal, but unpaid internships may offer academic credit or valuable skills. Utilize your college's career center or online job boards to find internship listings, and consider applying to multiple positions to increase your chances of securing one.

Freelancing

If you have skills in writing, graphic design, programming, or other areas, consider freelancing. Websites like Upwork, Freelancer, Fiverr, and various others allow you to create a profile and bid on projects. Start by offering your services at competitive rates and gradually increase your rates as you gain experience and build a portfolio.

Campus Opportunities

Explore various opportunities available on campus, such as becoming a resident assistant (RA), participating in paid research studies, or working as a campus tour guide. These positions often offer flexibility and may come with additional perks like housing or meal plans.

Tutoring

If you excel in a particular subject, consider offering tutoring services to other students. You can advertise your services through bulletin boards, campus newsletters, or online platforms. Tutoring can be a lucrative way to earn extra income while helping fellow students succeed academically.

Babysitting or Pet Sitting

Babysitting or pet sitting can be flexible and rewarding part-time jobs. Many families in college towns are looking for responsible people to care for their children or pets. Consider joining online platforms to find opportunities in your area.

Financial Aid Options and Scholarships

FAFSA (Free Application for Federal Student Aid)

Complete the FAFSA as soon as possible each year to determine your eligibility for federal grants, loans, and work-study programs. Colleges and universities use the information provided on the FAFSA to determine your financial aid package.

Grants and Scholarships

Research and apply for grants and scholarships offered by your college or university, private organizations, or government agencies. Look for scholarships specific to your field of study, ethnicity, extracurricular activities, or other criteria. Make your search thorough and apply to as many scholarships as possible to maximize your chances of receiving financial aid.

Work-Study Programs

If you qualify for work-study through your FAFSA, consider participating in a work-study program. These programs provide part-time employment opportunities on or off campus, often related to your field of study. Work-study jobs typically offer flexible hours and may be more accommodating to your class schedule.

Employer Tuition Assistance

Check if your or your parents' employers offer tuition assistance programs. Some companies provide financial support for employees or their dependents pursuing higher education. Speak with your employer's HR department to inquire about available benefits and eligibility criteria.

Tuition Reimbursement Programs

Some employers offer tuition reimbursement programs as part of their benefits package. These programs reimburse employees for a portion of their tuition expenses incurred while pursuing further education. If you're working part-time or full-time while attending college, explore whether your employer offers tuition reimbursement and take advantage of this benefit.

Strategies for Minimizing Student Loan Debt

Borrow Only What You Need

When applying for student loans, borrow only the amount necessary to cover tuition, fees, and essential living expenses. Avoid borrowing more than you need to minimize your debt burden after graduation. Create a budget to estimate your expenses and borrow accordingly.

Explore Federal Loan Options First

Federal student loans typically offer lower interest rates and more flexible repayment options compared to private loans. Maximize your federal loan options before considering private loans. Federal loans also offer benefits like income-driven repayment plans, loan forgiveness programs, and deferment or forbearance options in case of financial hardship.

Make Interest Payments During School

If you have unsubsidized federal loans, consider making interest payments while you're still in school. Making interest payments can prevent interest from capitalizing and accruing additional debt. Even small payments can make a significant difference in reducing the overall cost of your loans.

Apply for Loan Forgiveness Programs

Investigate loan forgiveness programs available to graduates in certain fields or professions. Programs like Public Service Loan Forgiveness (PSLF) forgive federal student loan debt for borrowers who work in qualifying public service jobs and make 120 qualifying payments. Research eligibility requirements and consider pursuing a career that qualifies for loan forgiveness if applicable to your career goals.

Budget and Manage Expenses Wisely

Develop a budget to track your income and expenses and avoid unnecessary spending. Look for ways to cut costs, such as renting textbooks instead of buying them, cooking meals at home, and utilizing student discounts. Prioritize your spending on essential needs and allocate funds toward saving and debt repayment.

Plan for Repayment

Before graduating, research repayment options for your student loans and choose a repayment plan. Evaluate different repayment plans, such as standard repayment, income-driven repayment, and extended repayment, and choose the one that best fits your financial situation and goals. Use loan repayment calculators to estimate your monthly payments and total interest costs under different repayment scenarios.

By implementing these strategies and exploring various opportunities for earning extra income and accessing financial aid, you can minimize student loan debt and achieve greater financial stability while in college. Remember to prioritize your education, manage your finances wisely, and take advantage of available resources to support your academic and financial success.

Mastering the art of financial management is not only essential during your college years, but it also sets the stage for lifelong financial success and independence. By diligent budgeting, seeking out extra income opportunities, and making informed decisions about financial aid and student loans, you're not just navigating the financial challenges of college – you're developing invaluable skills that will serve you well throughout your entire life.

Financial independence is about more than just having enough money to cover your expenses; it's about having the knowledge and confidence to make smart financial choices that align with your goals and values. By taking control of your finances now, you're laying the groundwork for a future where you have the freedom to pursue your dreams, whether that's traveling the world, starting a business, or buying a home.

Moreover, the skills gained from managing money effectively extend far beyond college. Learning to budget, save, invest, and avoid debt will serve you in every aspect of your life, from managing your career to planning for retirement. These skills provide a sense of empowerment and security, enabling you to weather financial storms and seize opportunities as they arise.

So, as you navigate the journey through college and beyond, remember the importance of financial independence and the lasting impact of mastering money management skills. Embrace the opportunity to learn and grow, and know that by taking control of your finances today, you're investing in a brighter, more secure future for yourself.

Chapter 9: Internship Insights: Gaining Experience While in School

After reading this chapter, you'll learn everything you need to know about gaining job experience while you're still in college. You'll understand how internships are the key to setting yourself apart from other candidates in a highly competitive job market. You'll also find out how internships can help you capitalize on your strengths, improve the areas in which you fall short, and land jobs more easily in the future. This chapter serves as your go-to guide on finding internships relevant to your interests and field of study, determining whether an internship is right for your needs, and how to make the most out of your time there.

Find internships that are relevant to your interests and your field of study.
https://www.pexels.com/photo/top-view-photo-of-people-near-wooden-table-3183150/

The Importance of Internships

Internships are programs offered by organizations to help train and offer real job experiences to students and fresh graduates for a certain amount of time. An internship can last anywhere between a month and over a year, depending on the company and its terms. While internships are optional for many students, some universities require internships as part of graduation prerequisites.

The Job Market Is Becoming More Competitive

The job market is becoming more competitive by the day. The changing economy and globalization significantly impact it and increase candidate requirements and expectations set by employers. Globalization and the rise of remote and hybrid work environments grant employers a larger pool of potential hires from all around the world. Instead of competing with the talent pool in your city and the neighboring areas, everyone is now competing with talents from all corners of the world. This still applies to non-remote positions.

- **Easy Access to Global Talents**

In today's world, it's easier to move from one country to another for job opportunities due to the increased access to information, global talent programs, and the increased rate of seeking international education and training. The internet has facilitated job searches for individuals and provides access to global opportunities. You can now complete the entire application and interview procedures over the Internet and only move when your position is secure. Some countries implement programs that help attract talents from all across the globe to fill certain gaps in the job market. Many students also seek higher education and training programs abroad, which often lead to residency, post-graduation work permits, and job opportunities.

With more people to choose from, employers increase their standards to ensure that they hire the most qualified and promising applicants. Technological and economic changes also lead to shifts in skill requirements. Over time, some skills are deemed obsolete while others become extremely high in demand, causing employers to constantly update their requirements. This, along with globalization, can also lead to the creation of niche markets, causing employers to seek out candidates with specific skill sets and qualifications.

- **The Rise of Artificial Intelligence and Automation**

The rise of artificial intelligence and task automation has also caused employers to increase the requirements for workers. It's very hard to land a job nowadays if you lack critical and creative thinking abilities, problem-solving skills, and advanced technical skills. Globalization has also made it easier for companies to set up international supply chains for better business opportunities, quality assurance, and cost management, causing employers to hire employees who are experienced in working in culturally diverse and international environments.

These are all reasons why high school diplomas and even good college degrees won't cut it if you want to secure a good job offer. Gaining valuable job experiences while you're still in a university can be a great step toward building a successful career. Completing internships in companies that are well-known and relevant to your desired field can help you stand out when it's time to apply for full-time jobs after you graduate.

Internships Give You a Competitive Advantage

Whether your university requires you to get an internship or not, internships are highly recommended. If two people apply for a job, and one of them has prior work experience and the other doesn't, the employer will likely hire the former. In a world where students and young professionals feel the constant need for personal improvement, don't take any chances. Internships are a great way to demonstrate your work ethic, skills, capabilities, and commitment and highlight that you've received relevant training and experience.

They Give You Insight into the Job Market

Internships give you insights into the real working world, increase your exposure to opportunities for growth and development, expand your knowledge, and help you determine whether you're on the right career path. While the knowledge you gain in a university is invaluable, it still doesn't match up to the real thing. It is a prerequisite for excelling in your career, but it doesn't fully prepare you for every aspect of the market's dynamics.

Internships help you bridge the gap between the theoretical knowledge you gain in your courses and the practical application of this information. They offer a perspective into what your job is like, the opportunities for growth and promotion that are available, and whether it's the right path for you. For instance, if you study marketing and advertising, you might think that working in an agency, brainstorming ideas for ads, and working in production or creative direction are the most fun and interesting jobs out there. However, once you work in an agency, get to deal with clients, and realize that you often have to work late at night, incredibly early in the morning, or on the weekends, especially during high seasons, you might realize that you prefer to work in a more stable and predictable work environment. Others might be fine with the highly demanding nature of their industry, especially if they don't have many commitments or responsibilities other than work.

You should also make use of your time in college and try to complete several internships in different places. This will help you determine whether the things you like and dislike about work are company- or industry-related. For example, if you're worried that there is little room for promotion in your scope of work, you might've just interned in a small agency or company. Everything you learn during your internships will benefit you in your future jobs. Whether you understand the best ways to communicate with colleagues and clients, learn how to set boundaries at work, or expand your technical skills, these are all things that will benefit you in the future.

They Help You Expand Your Network

Internships are also great opportunities to expand your professional network before you graduate. If you prove yourself during the internship period, it can lead to better opportunities within the organization, such as a promise of a full-time job once you graduate – or even mentorship opportunities and references. Observing how professionals within your field approach challenges, interact with clients and other employees, accomplish their tasks, and achieve their goals efficiently will allow you to develop your own approach.

Internships Teach You about Your Interests and Capabilities

Internships also help you learn more about yourself and your interests. You'll never unlock your full range of skills, talents, and capabilities unless you find yourself in a real-world work environment. Internships will teach you about your strengths and weaknesses and allow you to put your technical, problem-solving, and critical-thinking skills to the test, especially in challenging situations. Internships give you insight into the areas in which you excel and the things that set you apart from others, as well as the areas in which you fall short. This way, you can capitalize on your strong areas and improve your shortcomings.

How to Find Relevant Internships

Identify Your Goals and Interests

When searching for internships, you need to identify your interests and career goals. This will allow you to determine the type of internship you want to search for. You should also create a list of your requirements, including the duration, location, and compensation. Depending on your field, you might struggle to land a paid internship. In that case, you might want to apply for one either way to gain experience, make connections, and improve your resume.

If compensation is important, you can seek out part-time opportunities. When browsing through internships, you must also consider your expectations, the types of programs the companies are offering, the job description, and the type of responsibilities you'll have. Ideally, internships should be interesting and offer opportunities for learning and growth. The size of the company is also something you should consider. In most cases, large companies have a clearer division of responsibilities and job descriptions, while smaller ones offer more hands-on experiences.

Get a Headstart on the Search

Like the full-time job market, internships can be extremely competitive. Most companies have application deadlines, so don't put off your search until the last minute. Regularly check job boards, the websites, and social media of companies you're interested in to stay on top of updates.

Make Use of Your Resources

Use the available resources to find the right internship for you.
https://www.pexels.com/photo/pondering-woman-working-on-modern-laptop-in-living-room-7015074/

- **Online Research**

    If you're already interested in specific companies, research whether they have internship programs and when and how to apply. Verse yourself on the requirements and application processes. If you can't find information online, email the department you want to work for, explain that you're interested in interning there and why, and attach your resume. Taking this step shows your dedication and willingness to work with them.

- **Job Search Platforms and College Career Centers**

    Use online job search platforms to find internships. You can filter your results by location, industry, position, and start date for the most accurate findings. You can also use your school's career center, check your student email regularly, and browse through updated internship-related documents, if available, to facilitate the search. Most universities reach out to both companies and alumni to offer career and learning opportunities for students.

- **Local Career Centers and Career Fairs**

    You can also consider getting in touch with local career centers or attending career fairs to network with potential employers. Before you go, however, prepare an elevator pitch about yourself to highlight the value you'll bring to the workplace. Keep several copies of your resume with you, and make sure to talk to the representatives while you're there to determine whether the companies you're interested in are a good fit for you.

- **Your Personal and Professional Networks**

    Take the time to review your professional and personal networks to find people who might help you gain experience in your desired field. Chances are that you know someone who knows someone who would be willing to give you insights into the industry and even help you land an opportunity through referrals.

How to Choose the Right Internship

Consider Your Interests and Desired Career Path

When choosing an internship, make sure that it aligns with your interests and your desired industry and area of study. If you're going to work alongside your academics, then make it worth your while. Choose job opportunities that will add value to your resume.

You should choose a company and position that you're actually interested in working at – and one where you're certain to learn new skills and gain new knowledge. Before choosing an internship, think about why you want it, what you want to learn from it, how it will help you advance in your career, and whether you need to meet certain requirements to be accepted for it. You should also consider the time you need to dedicate to this job, how much time it's going to take to get there, and the responsibilities you'll have.

Consider Your University's Requirements

Make sure to check with your university to see if they have any requirements regarding your internship. Some universities require that you complete internships in certain positions or companies or have a certain GPA before interning or working part-time. Avoid going against any of your university's guidelines to receive your degree on time. Check with your counselor before choosing an internship to ensure that it will be accepted. You should also make sure you understand the stipulations of your internship. Find out beforehand whether you'll get paid or receive college credit.

Balance Your Work and Academic Hours

If you're going to complete your internship during your academic semester rather than during the summer break, be sure to consider the working hours beforehand. For instance, if you're required to work at times when you have classes, don't take the internship. You shouldn't compromise your academic performance in order to pursue an internship. Seek companies that offer part-time positions or flexible working hours to avoid interfering with your academic schedule.

Understand the Organizational Culture

Each company has a unique culture and work environment. Get to know the companies you're eyeing to ensure that you'll enjoy your time there. You'll only make the most of your internship when the people around you are willing to help and offer valuable information. Know the difference between private sector, public sector, and non-profit organizations to determine the right one for your needs.

Consider the Location and Commute

The location of your internship is also a major deciding factor when you're choosing a place to work in. You don't want to spend a lot of time transporting to and from the company. It might not be too bothersome at first; however, keeping it up for a long while can result in commute stress.

How to Make the Most of Your Internship

1. **Get to know your coworkers.** Make sure to introduce yourself to everyone in your department as soon as you get there. Build rapport with them and show interest in what they do. Set a favorable first impression to make them more likely to help you further down the line. Even if you don't plan on working in this company after you graduate, you can ask for recommendations from them. The harder you work, the more memorable you'll be to your team and supervisor.

2. **Align with the company's goals.** If they don't set a meeting for you, ask to meet with your supervisor when you start your internship to find out what they expect from you throughout your duration there. Ask them what you're supposed to accomplish every day, who you'll receive your tasks from and submit them to, where to receive help and feedback whenever you need it, and how you'll know whether you're on the right track. Most importantly, don't lose sight of your own objectives and things that you'd like to work on. Discuss your expectations and interests to ensure they involve you in relevant learning opportunities.

3. **Observe and reach out for help.** Even after you graduate and have substantial work experience, you'll never walk into a new company and immediately understand how everything is done. Understanding the organizational culture is key to succeeding in a new work environment. Observe how your coworkers interact and get things done. Familiarize yourself with the organizational routines and procedures, read all relevant material, and don't hesitate to ask for help and guidance whenever you need it. Whenever possible, jump on opportunities to attend meetings and other important events.

4. **Maintain professionalism.** Even if you're only an intern, maintaining high levels of professionalism and being mindful of how you present yourself to everyone in the organization can set you apart. Respect the dress code, email etiquette, and company standard procedures. Determine the right person to report to and talk to whenever you have a problem so you don't

go over their head. Maintain basic manners and courtesy at all times as well.

5. **Keep busy.** If you submit all your tasks and have nothing else to do, let your supervisor know that things are slow for you. If they have nothing else for you to do, read about your industry and its updates, and ask your supervisor and coworkers if it's okay to help others when needed. If you're in a creative field, you can come up with ideas for long-term projects and suggest them to your supervisor. For instance, if you work in marketing, you can draft ideas for events or campaigns that can help your company gain traction. Going beyond your job description and showing your enthusiasm to learn can help you land a full-time position or receive a strong recommendation from your employers.

6. **Stay organized and manage your time effectively.** Whenever you attend a meeting, even if it's informal, make sure you take detailed notes, create to-do lists, and mark down deadlines to stay on top of tasks. Get things done on time and ask for more tasks when you finish the ones at hand. However, be careful not to bite off more than you can chew to avoid slacking. If you're feeling overwhelmed, ask your supervisor about which tasks to prioritize. Keep your workspace organized because it helps you get things done more efficiently and sets a favorable impression. Keep your data stored neatly so you and those who need them can access them with ease. Follow data storage and record maintenance policies whenever applicable.

Internships allow you to learn from experienced professionals and determine whether your desired career path is right for you. You'll gain exposure to the job market, different work environments, and organizational cultures and build a strong network of professional connections who can help you land permanent jobs in the future or give you strong referrals.

Chapter 10: Senior Year Sprint: Preparing for Life after Graduation

After graduation, you'll arrive at yet another crucial turning point in your life. This period often comes with mixed feelings for college students. On the one hand, you are happy that you're at the end of your college journey and about to enter into the professional life. On the other hand, you'll become aware that your life, including your social circle, will change. Moreover, you'll be under pressure to make the right choices to establish the path toward a successful and fulfilling future.

After graduation, you'll arrive at yet another crucial turning point in your life.
https://www.pexels.com/photo/photography-of-people-graduating-1205651/

Because the senior year is a pivotal time for reflection and forward planning, this chapter will focus on navigating the challenges college students face as they approach the end of their college journey. This transitional phase can be challenging, but embracing it is all the more crucial for long-term success. Besides tips for career planning and finding your first job, the chapter also offers tips for budgeting after graduation, navigating student loans, honing essential skills, and more.

Career Planning

Having a career objective as a fresh graduate is useful, but there are other aspects to consider in your future career planning. For example, you may have a job lined up after graduation and assume that you'll work there for many years afterward. But what happens if you lose that job or realize that your dream vacation isn't on the trajectory of that career path? Here are a few useful tips for successful career planning that guarantee satisfaction in the long run.

Practice Self-Assessment

A thorough self-assessment, such as a SWOT analysis (standing for Strengths, Weaknesses, Opportunities, and Threats), will help you identify the skills you have, need, and need to improve. Start by revealing abilities that would make you a valuable employee and figuring out your key points of improvement. You can do both by asking colleagues, mentors, and other associates for feedback on your work skills.

Then, look for opportunities and pitfalls that may be outside your control when looking for a job after graduation. This can include avenues for advancing your career in the chosen field, professional growth, and anything that can hinder this.

Weigh in Your Options

If you wish to find an industry where you can work for the next five to 10 years, start by exploring the options. When analyzing the different industries, make sure to also look at how they interact with each other. It's okay to chase your passions, but these might change, and if you can find an industry that lets you transition into another one when needed, all the better. It will help you avoid burnout and stress.

Plan Long-Term

Think about where you want to be in seven to 10 years. Do you see yourself in a specific position at a company? Or, perhaps you want to focus on acquiring specific skills and experiences in an industry. Either way, with this long-term goal in mind, you can devise a roadmap toward your dream and look for a job that lays the foundational step toward it.

Find a Mentor

If you have a specific career objective in mind, finding a mentor who can answer crucial questions about getting to your dream job will help you get started on the right path. A mentor from the same profession can help you make connections in the industry. The easiest way to find a mentor is to either join an online mentorship platform or connect to them through social media (there are sites dedicated to linking professionals from the same and different industries).

Learn to Network

College presents plenty of opportunities to build networks that not only benefit you personally but also professionally. Capitalizing on your existing networks is one of the most efficient ways to kickstart your career after graduation. There are plenty of free networking events college students can take advantage of and connect with people who have the skills and expertise needed in the professional world.

Job Search Strategies

Here are some more concrete strategies for finding the right job after graduation.

Gain Experience during College

Lots of students have jobs during college, which allows them to gain experience they can use to obtain a job after graduation. However, just because you didn't work during college, you can still gain experience from participating in the work of different organizations or clubs, attending seminars, and other avenues for acquiring new skills.

Pro tip: If you didn't have a job during college, use your participation in a club or organization as your job experience.

Put Your Network to Use

The network you've built during college can help you find jobs that may not be advertised. These may be friends or family, but also coworkers, a professional organization, or individuals. Moreover, if you apply for a job at a company, having someone in your network who works for the company will raise your chances of landing the job. You can reach out to them for references or tips on how to secure the job.

Research the Market

Researching the different work opportunities can help you narrow down the search. For example, you can look into what a typical day at a job would look like at the different companies and positions you're considering, seeing whether it'll be a good fit for you. Likewise, exploring the requirements and the rate for career development in the different industries will help you understand what the companies are looking for and help you prepare to showcase the skills that ensure you land the job.

Be Proactive

If you're like most college students, you'll have student loans and other finances to juggle, which means you'll need to find employment right after you graduate. To do this, you need to be proactive. Start by applying for several different positions, and don't forget to follow up on applications you haven't heard back on. Contact the hiring managers and let them know you're still interested and reinforce why you would be a suitable fit for the position. By doing this, you're showing them that you're a professional ready to put your talents and skills to work.

Volunteer

Volunteering isn't only a marvelous way to give back to the community – it's also a great avenue for developing and honing your skills. It's particularly beneficial for enhancing interpersonal and communication skills, which will come in handy during your job interviews.

Attend Career Fairs

Career fairs are excellent opportunities to find recruiters who might be interested in learning about your skills and experience. Make sure to research companies attending the fair so you can prepare specific questions to ask the representatives.

Find an Internship

Even if you can't get a job right away, landing a paid internship will help you establish yourself at a company. After completing the internship, you'll have higher chances of landing the job, and often with a higher starting salary, too, than those without internship experience. Taking an internship is also another way to build your skills, even if you can't turn it into a full-time position. It can still help you find a higher-salary job afterward because you'll have valuable experience.

Get a Part-Time Job

Like an internship, a part-time job can help you get started in the field. It fosters building connections, work ethic, and experience, and it allows you to earn money to contribute to your finances. Working at a part-time job will help you understand your work style and what you enjoy or don't enjoy doing at your work.

Leverage Campus Career Services

Like job fairs, campus career centers are excellent sources of employment opportunities. They can help you find a job locally, even after graduation. Employers who leave their information in the career centers often have specific requirements, like experience in a particular field. If you've obtained these skills through part-time jobs, internships, or even volunteer jobs, you'll have a higher chance of getting hired by these companies.

Take Online Courses

Another way to expand your skill set beyond what you've acquired in college is to take online courses. You'll gain experience and a chance to land higher-paying jobs. A tip: Take advantage of free online courses to save money in your budget.

Establish a Routine

Job hunting after college may seem like a daunting prospect, but a routine will make everything go more smoothly and help you achieve your goals. This job-seeking routine can include the following:

- Updating your resume
- Searching for jobs
- Applying for jobs
- Following up with hiring managers and recruiters
- Networking
- Building your skills

Make sure to also include breaks to relieve the stress that comes with the process. This could be anything from going on a walk or run to doing a self-care ritual to watching a movie.

Apply to Companies Directly

Even if a company isn't hiring when you're looking for a job, it doesn't hurt to reach out and show interest in working for them. Some companies even have dedicated forms on their websites through which potential candidates can apply, even when they don't have current openings but plan to have them in the future.

Transitioning into the Professional World

Transitioning from college to the professional world can be challenging, whether because you're adjusting to a new schedule, leaving your social circle (roommates and friends you've spent most of your time on campus with), trying to find employment, or comparing your success in this field to others.

Here are a few tips to help you get through this period:
- Acknowledge your transition, even if it isn't the smoothest, instead of beating yourself up if things don't go as planned.
- Keep working on establishing professional connections.
- If you find a job, don't be afraid to ask for more responsibilities if you think you can handle them (it shows dedication).
- Prepare to work in an entry-level position.
- Create a new schedule that accommodates your new responsibilities.
- Devise an alternative career plan – in case your existing one doesn't work out.
- Continue working on your soft (personality-related) and hard (learned) skills.
- Cultivate your professionalism while applying for jobs (it will come in handy when you land one).

Life Skills You'll Need after College

Transitioning into the professional world requires working on skills and experiences, including financial planning, independent living, continuing education, student loan repayment, understanding employee benefits, basic budgeting, and more.

Cultivating life skills is necessary, especially after college.
https://www.pexels.com/photo/photo-of-people-doing-handshakes-3183197/

Cultivating Passion

Whether you can land a job that aligns with your career vision right away or not, it's crucial to keep cultivating your passion. If you already have what helps you grow your skills and interests, then empowering your passion toward it will make it easier to advance. If you've taken the job because it was the only offer you got, identifying what you're passionate about will help you work toward the career path that you wish to follow in the future.

Learning the Importance of Goal Setting

Both short- and long-term goals will challenge you to expand and hone your skills. Reaching them will motivate you to strive for bigger achievements. Remember, measure your goals to your abilities. Don't compare yourself to others because your paths may be different, and self-criticism will only deter you from your goals.

Embracing Failure

Failure is part of life, and you'll inevitably encounter bad luck or make a mistake that will cost you time, effort, and money. If you're passionate about something and hit a brick wall, you'll be confronted with an enormous sense of failure. Use this as fuel for learning how to circumvent the challenge next time around.

Becoming Open to Criticism

While most students deal with criticism from professors, they'll likely face far more at the workplace. For some people, it's not easy to handle. However, instead of becoming defensive, try to see feedback and constructive criticism as learning opportunities.

Understanding Workplace Etiquette

You'll likely learn that the workplace is far from the casual environment you experienced at college. Even if your employer offers a relaxed work environment, you'll still benefit from workplace etiquette, showcasing professionalism and timeliness.

Cultivating Patience

Unlike many other things in this fast-paced world, professional accomplishments rarely come rapidly. Expecting immediate results will only lead to a stronger sense of failure. Arm yourself with patience and be prepared to work toward your goals.

Identifying Your Definition of Success

When you start to transition into professional life, you must figure out what success means to you. This may mean landing a certain position, gaining experience, or building a network of people you can work with. Whatever your definition of success is, having a clear definition of it in your mind's eye will encourage you to work toward it.

Money Management

You'll be faced with many financial responsibilities, from managing your student loans to creating smart budgets for adequate fund distribution.

Student Loan Repayment

For starters, it's a good idea to create a loan payment plan to start working on eradicating your student loan debt. Follow these steps when creating and following the repayment plan:

- Track your lender, balance, and repayment status for each of your student loans, as these details will determine your repayment and forgiveness options.
- Familiarize yourself with your grace periods: Grace periods (the period you have after finishing school before you must start repaying the loan) differ from one loan to another.
- Stay in touch with the lender: Maintain communication with the lender, including via email and phone. If you change any of your contact information, make sure to notify the lender. Otherwise, it can end up costing you more money.
- Choose the right repayment option: The standard option for federal loans is a 10-year repayment plan; however, you may be able to extend this period. By doing so, you can lower your monthly payments but incur higher interest. Other options include income-driven repayment plans (IDR), which allow for a cap on your company payment based on a certain percentage of your annual income. Private loans come with different options, and it's best to consult with your lender about their repayment.
- Don't panic if you run into problems: If you can't make your payments due to medical issues, loss of employment, or other financial challenges, try to find out what other option you have for managing your student loans. For federal loans, this may include forbearance or deferment, both of which are a lifesaver in times of short-term hardships, but they come with higher interest.
- Don't ignore your loans: Ignoring your debt can result in default, which has a negative effect on your credit score and raises the total amount you owe drastically. After nine months of non-payment, the government can seize your tax refunds and wages to satisfy your debt on federal loans. Private lenders have an even shorter tolerance period.
- Look into loan forgiveness options: Various programs will forgive all or some of your federal student loans if you work in certain fields or for certain types of employers.

Building your Credit

The higher your credit score is, the more likely you are to get a lower rate on a credit card or loan. It can even help you get approved for apartments. Your credit score is determined based on your accounts and financial history. You can build your credit by paying your student loans and current bills on time, as well as managing your credit card balance smartly. If you don't yet have bills in your name, you can start building your credit by signing up for a low-limit credit card.

Emergency Funds and Other Protection

The easiest way to establish an emergency fund is to accumulate enough money in your savings account to cover three to six months of your monthly expenses. This will give you peace of mind in case of an emergency or unexpected expenses.

Beyond savings, another way to cover yourself for emergencies is to get adequate insurance, like health insurance, homeowners or renters insurance, and disability insurance.

Creating a Monthly Income Plan

Budgeting your income will help you meet your obligations, track your spending, and start saving. Create a list of your total income and obligations to get the full picture of your finances.

Understanding Employee Benefits

Among the factors to consider when looking for employment are the employee benefits. These can vary by company, but it's a good idea to familiarize yourself with the basic terms and information to know what to look for in a potential employer benefit package.

For example, did you know that some companies have a waiting period between when you begin working and when the benefits kick in? Typically, this is the first of the month after 30 days of working.

The benefits will be deducted from your paycheck based on what benefit you choose. To choose adequate insurance, consider your current health needs and prospective future needs and research your options.

Here are a few medical benefit-related terms to know:

- HDHP (High Deductible Health Plan) enables you to pay a discounted rate (without co-pay) for services until you meet your deductible.
- PPO (Preferred Provider Organization) allows for paying co-pays for doctor visits and prescriptions until you meet your deductible (comes with higher monthly premiums and out-of-pocket costs).
- With a HSA (Health Savings Account), you can set aside pre-tax income into a savings account for medical expenses.
- The deductible is the amount you pay for medical expenses out of pocket before the insurance kicks in.
- The premium is the amount you pay per month for your insurance coverage (it's the regular amount deducted from your paycheck).
- Out-of-pocket is the (usually limited) amount you pay each year for healthcare, including co-pays, deductibles, and coinsurance.
- In-network or out-of-network is the term used to distinguish health care providers accepting your insurance plan and those they don't (at the latter, you'll pay a higher rate for services).
- Open enrollment is the period when you can enroll in benefits for the subsequent year (it's a good idea to elect your benefits during this time or when you're hired).
- Qualifying events are those that make it possible to enroll in benefits outside open enrollment (for example, the birth of a child, marriage, divorce, death of a dependent, a spouse losing their group benefits, or a child no longer being covered by their parent's insurance after a certain age).
- Dental insurance covers dental healthcare needs, including services from regular cleanings to major dental work.
- Vision insurance covers any vision healthcare need, including regular checkups, glasses, and contacts.
- Other benefit terms to familiarize yourself with include:
- Disability insurance: You can rely on this when a medical issue prevents you from being able to work and earn a salary. It can either be short- or long-term.
- Paid time off and holidays: The former can include personal days, sick days, and vacation days, and the amount can vary from one employer to another, as can your schedule. Holidays also depend on the employer's policy, as some choose to cease working during holidays while

others stay open depending on the nature of the industry.
- **Wellness:** More and more employers are offering wellness programs to their employees. These can include anything from covering gym membership fees to other wellness-related activities you can attend, courtesy of your employer.
- Some companies also offer education reimbursement. Depending on the industry or employer, you may receive reimbursement for your tuition fees for continued education, certification costs, and more.
- 401(k) is a contribution plan funded by employers. It enables you to set aside tax-free income for retirement purposes. You may need to contribute a portion on your own, and the employer will match this amount. If they don't, and you're the only one paying for your 401(k), then all of the money you contributed must be paid to you when you stop working at the company.
- Maternity or paternity leave is the time mothers and fathers receive upon the birth or adoption of a child. The leave can either be paid or unpaid.
- Extras like paid parking and free or discounted food, products, and services are perks that increase employee satisfaction.

Pending responsibilities notwithstanding, try not to worry about your future too much. The key to a successful transition lies in finding the balance between preparation for life after graduation and savoring your college years. After all, it's a unique experience – one full of opportunities for professional and personal growth.

Whether you have prospects outlined for the future or not, with a proactive approach and dedication, you'll be able to achieve your dreams. In the meantime, remember that having fun with friends, socializing, and partaking in enjoyable activities are just as important for a healthy and happy life as establishing the foundation of your future career.

Conclusion

In the future, your college years will become the most memorable years of your life. Make those memories fond and cherished by following this guide, but don't hesitate to experiment on your own with new things. Every aspect of your college life, both the good things and the bad, will build your future and shape you into the person you wish to be.

In summary, you started with your freshman year, which may be easy to get through but hard to thrive in. Peer pressure will probably be your biggest hurdle. The key is to learn from your mistakes. That is how you will evolve and eventually be able to solve all your problems.

College is all about new experiences, and studies form an integral part of those. Your courses will be more interesting and advanced, but they will be based on the fundamentals you learned in high school. Take a refresher course if your fundamentals aren't strong enough. Effective time management techniques are essential for maintaining high grades throughout.

You learned how to handle any possible problem in your living space. Understanding and navigating dorm room diplomacy is critical to making your college life outside the campus easier. If you cannot be friends with your roommates, maintain mutual respect and don't cross the agreed-upon boundaries.

At most colleges in the U.S., food is easy to come by. They have dedicated cafeterias for students, and many food trucks prefer to park near the school during lunchtime. You will be spoiled with choices, so it's important to develop a strict diet to maintain your health. Setting food reminders on your phone helps when the coursework is intense and you forget to eat.

Then, you came to the most alluring aspect of college life - having fun. Unless you are having fun studying, keep these two aspects of your college life separate. Participate in different activities and explore your creative potential, but don't let it affect your grades. Competitive activities coupled with studies can increase your stress. Follow stress-busting methods like meditation and working out.

With a new environment comes new friends. You learned how to deal with the anxieties of making new friends with fun activities like the "Social Interaction Challenge." Then, you proceeded to acquire the power of budget management. Your new friends' lifestyles and your own desires may prompt you to spend more than you can afford. It's crucial to curb that urge.

The final pages took you through the final stages of your college life, including internships and your senior year. You then learned that this is the time for you to shift your focus toward your goals to carve a bright future for yourself.

If you enjoyed this book, I'd greatly appreciate a review on Amazon because it helps me to create more books that people want. It would mean a lot to hear from you.

To leave a review:
1. Open your camera app.
2. Point your mobile device at the QR code.
3. The review page will appear in your web browser.

_____

Thanks for your support!

Check out another book in the series

References

10 challenges you may encounter at university | Undergraduate Programs. (2023, June 1). Undergraduate Programs. https://uwaterloo.ca/future-students/missing-manual/student-life/10-challenges-you-may-encounter-university

Adjusting to College - Office of Counseling and Health Services. (n.d.). Office of Counseling and Health Services. https://drexel.edu/counselingandhealth/counseling-center/students/adjustment/

Admin. (2022, March 21). The Importance of Self-Care. Winds of Change. https://woc.aises.org/content/importance-self-care

Johnson, M. (2023, April 12). Making Friends in College: Vital to Your Success. Cleveland University-Kansas City. https://www.cleveland.edu/making-friends-in-college-vital-to-your-success/

Lparsons. (2022, November 9). 8 Time Management Tips for Students - Harvard Summer School. Harvard Summer School. https://summer.harvard.edu/blog/8-time-management-tips-for-students/

Tychr. (2023, September 15). College Life: Navigating the Challenges and Opportunities. TYCHR. https://tychr.com/college-life-navigating-the-challenges-and-opportunities/

Wood, S. (2022, June 27). Don't Make These 8 Mistakes as a College Freshman. US News & World Report. https://www.usnews.com/education/best-colleges/articles/dont-make-these-mistakes-as-a-college-freshman

Arias, A. (2023, August 24). 5 Common Roommate Fights & How to Solve Them, According to an RA. Dorm Therapy. https://www.dormtherapy.com/college-roommate-fights-solve-ra-advice-100001397

BigFuture. (2024). College Roommates: The Basics – BigFuture | College Board. Bigfuture.collegeboard.org. https://bigfuture.collegeboard.org/plan-for-college/college-basics/campus-life/college-roommates-the-basics

Bonner, M. (2018, May 17). Roommate 101: How to Live in Harmony With Your Roomie | napCincinnati. NAP. https://apartments.naproperties.com/nap-cincinnati/blog/roommate-101-how-to-live-in-harmony-with-your-roomie

Brinson, L. C. (2012, August 8). 5 House Rules to Set with Your Dorm Roommate. HowStuffWorks. https://home.howstuffworks.com/community-living/5-house-rules-set-dorm-roommate.htm

Caitlin. (2014, February 11). How to live in peace with a roommate: 8 tips. Moveline. https://www.moveline.com/blog/how-to-live-in-peace-with-a-roommate-8-tips

Erb, S. E., Renshaw, K. D., Short, J. L., & Pollard, J. W. (2014). The Importance of College Roommate Relationships: A Review and Systemic Conceptualization. Journal of Student Affairs Research and Practice, 51(1), 43–55. https://doi.org/10.1515/jsarp-2014-0004

Fisher, T. (2020, September 23). Resolution Strategies for Roommate Conflict | Alcove Blog. Alcoverooms.com. https://alcoverooms.com/blog/post/resolution-strategies-for-roommate-conflicts

Fuson, F., & Fuson, M. (2023). College Roommate Essentials on How To Talk To Anyone: The Ultimate Survival Guide on How to Have Roommates That Don't Suck! In R. Peace (Ed.), Amazon. Harmony. https://www.amazon.com/College-Roommate-Essentials-Talk-Anyone/dp/0985938196

Kelly, J., & Bowen, L. (2021, August 4). How to Live in Harmony with Your Roommate. The Crimson White. https://thecrimsonwhite.com/82226/culture/how-to-live-in-harmony-with-your-roommate/

Parel, A. (2016, August 9). 9 College Freshman Fears (And How to Face Them). The Odyssey Online. https://www.theodysseyonline.com/9-college-freshman-fears-face-them

Smith, B. (2018, January 25). 4 Ways To Develop Better Relationships With Your College Roommates 1/25. The Odyssey Online. https://www.theodysseyonline.com/build-better-relationships-college-roommates

Wallace, L. (2023, October 27). Living the Sweet Dorm Life: 8 Roommate Communication Tips. Www.collegexpress.com. https://www.collegexpress.com/articles-and-advice/student-life/articles/living-campus/living-the-sweet-dorm-life-8-roommate-communication-tips/

Zumper. (2021, January 5). 13 Essential Roommate Rules That Will Make Your Lives Easier. The Zumper Blog. https://www.zumper.com/blog/roommate-rules/

Bandurski, K. (2022, February 10). 40 Healthy Recipes Any College Student Can Master. Taste of Home. https://www.tasteofhome.com/collection/easy-healthy-college-meals/

How College Students Benefit From Healthy Meal Plans. (2021, August 17). American Dining Creations. https://adc-us.com/blog/how-college-students-benefit-from-healthy-meal-plans/

Johnson, J. (2023, June 5). Food on Campus Can Promote Sociability and Understanding. American Enterprise Institute - AEI. https://www.aei.org/society-and-culture/food-on-campus-can-promote-sociability-and-understanding/

The Grubhub Staff. (2023, July 6). Using Food to Elevate the College Experience. Grubhub Onsite. https://onsite.grubhub.com/blog/using-food-to-elevate-the-college-experience/

Welshans, M. (2023, March 13). 7 Tips for Navigating Your College Dining Hall. Lancaster General Health.org. https://www.lancastergeneralhealth.org/health-hub-home/2023/march/7-tips-for-navigating-your-college-dining-hall

Dumoski, S. (2022, February 3). 5 steps for making friends in college. Chapman Newsroom. https://news.chapman.edu/2022/02/03/5-steps-for-making-friends-in-college/

How to make friends at college in the US. (n.d.). Shorelight.com. https://shorelight.com/student-stories/how-to-make-friends-in-college-tips-for-international-students/

How to make friends in college: 5 practical tips. (n.d.). Stjohns.edu https://www.stjohns.edu/news-media/johnnies-blog/%20/how-to-make-friends-in-college

How to make new friends in college. (n.d.). Mohawk College. https://www.mohawkcollege.ca/about/news/blogs/how-to-make-new-friends-college

Paonita, J. (2022, November 13). How to make friends in college (even if you're shy). The Scholarship System; The Scholarship System LLC. https://thescholarshipsystem.com/blog-for-students-families/how-to-make-friends-in-college-even-if-youre-shy/

10 Tips to Make the Most of an Internship | Columbia CCE. (n.d.). https://www.careereducation.columbia.edu/resources/10-tips-make-most-internship

How to Choose the Right Internship. (n.d.). Arkansas State University. https://www.astate.edu/a/global-initiatives/online/a-state-online-services/online-career-center/resources/How%20to%20Choose%20the%20Right%20Internship.pdf

How to Find an Internship That Matters - BigFuture. (n.d.). https://bigfuture.collegeboard.org/plan-for-college/college-prep/stand-out/how-to-find-an-internship-youll-value

Indeed, Editorial Team. (2023, June 9). 9 Best Ways To Find an Internship (and Why It's Important). Indeed.com. https://www.indeed.com/career-advice/finding-a-job/how-to-find-internships

Vinay. (2023, November 16). The importance of an internship: 5 critical reasons. Capital Placement. https://capital-placement.com/blog/the-importance-of-an-internship-top-5-reasons-why-internships-are-critical/

Anders. (2020, September 11). Understanding Employee Benefits: A Guide for Recent Graduates. Anders CPA. https://anderscpa.com/understanding-employee-benefits-guide-for-recent-graduates/

Du, M. (2022, July 12). 7 Steps To Planning Your Career After Graduation. Prosple Philippines. https://ph.prosple.com/career-planning/7-steps-to-planning-your-career-after-graduation

Hanson, B. (2024, February 8). 17 game-changing tips for getting a job after college. Intuit Credit Karma. https://www.creditkarma.com/income/i/how-to-get-job-after-college

Indeed, Editorial Team. (2022, June 25). 11 Tips for Transitioning from College to the Workplace. Indeed. https://www.indeed.com/career-advice/career-development/transitioning-from-college-to-workplace

Markarian, T. (2022, December 19). 14 Life Tips Every Recent Grad Needs to Have in Their Back Pocket. Reader's Digest. https://www.rd.com/list/life-skills-recent-college-grad/

Members 1st. (2023, June 23). Budgeting Tips for New College Grads | M1st. Www. members 1st.org. https://www.members1st.org/blog/articles/budgeting-for-new-college-grads/

The Top 10 Student Loan Tips for Recent Graduates. (n.d.). The Institute for College Access & Success. https://ticas.org/for-students-parents/the-top-10-student-loan-tips-for-recent-graduates

www.ingramcontent.com/pod-product-compliance
Lightning Source LLC
Chambersburg PA
CBHW081353040426

42450CB00016B/3429